Clans
and
Tartans

THE FABRIC OF SCOTLAND

Lord Duffus by Richard Waitt. The noble lord is wearing his clan tartan, the Sutherland. Although he was originally a supporter of the 1707 Union with England, Lord Duffus defected to the Jacobites in 1715. He fled to Sweden, but returned to Britain and was imprisoned in the Tower of London. Released in 1717, he joined the Imperial Russian navy, and rose to the rank of admiral.

CLaNs
and
TaRTaNs

THE FABRIC OF SCOTLAND

L O R N A   B L A C K I E

the
apple
press

A QUINTET BOOK

Published by Apple Press Ltd
293 Gray's Inn Road,
London WC1X 8QF

ISBN 0-85076-091-8

This book was designed and produced by
Quintet Publishing Limited
6 Blundell Street
London N7 9BH

Art Director: Peter Bridgewater
Editors: Sonya Mills, Josephine Bacon
Picture Researcher: Anne-Marie Ehrlich

The author and publishers would like to thank
Mr Harry Lindley, Kinloch Anderson Ltd.,
Edinburgh for his valuable assistance.

Colour photographs of all tartans except those on
pages 11, 14(l), 39(r) and 55(l) © copyright
Strawberry Hill Press Limited, 1987. Unauthorized
reproduction of these photographs is forbidden.

Other photographs courtesy of: E.T. Archive:
pages 7, 9, 10; Scottish National Gallery:
pages 2, 12; MacArthur Memorial, Norfolk,
Virginia: page 12

Typeset in Great Britain by
QV Typesetting Limited, 6 Blundell Street,
London N7 9BH
Manufactured in Hong Kong by Regent
Publishing Services Limited
Printed in Hong Kong by Leefung-Asco Printers
Limited

contents

Out of the Celtic myths and mists came the wandering close-knit tribes of the Irish Celts who called themselves Scots. They crossed the sea and settled on the mainland of Britain, north of the firths of Forth and Clyde, the bleak wilderness that the Romans had named Caledonia. The geographer Ptolemy wrote that even by the 2nd century A.D., there were thirteen tribes in unconquered Caledonia, the land that would later be known as Scotland.

The Celts brought with them not only a rich oral and written culture but also an extraordinarily powerful perception of their racial kinship and blood-ties; and later, despite their nomadic origins, there developed in them an equally strong feeling for the lands on which they had settled.

These deep attachments to soil and tribe were the emotional foundations of the unique Scottish clan system that was to evolve, in which free men pledged their first loyalties to their their kith and kin and to their patriarchal leader — even to the death.

In its many centuries of existence the clan system has suffered disruption by marauding barbarians, it has been repressed and outlawed by greedy foreign kings and it has been weakened by poverty and the enforced dispersal of its members into exile. But its continuity has never been broken and it thrives today.

The story of the clans is a strange, sometimes mysterious and often bloody tale, but it is also an inspiring one, with perhaps some lessons for our own cynical times in which concepts like loyalty, kinship and pride of birthplace are too often spoken of in terms of derision.

The associated story of the clans' tartans is no less fascinating and is by no means a minor part of the whole. To a clansman his tartan is a great deal more than a mere preference in dress. It is a powerful symbol of his clan loyalties and clan history, a tribal uniform endowed with a deep significance for all who are entitled to wear it.

This potent symbolism was fully understood by the government in London which in 1746, after the battle of Culloden, as part of an attempt to stamp out the recalcitrant Highland culture, proscribed the wearing of clan dress. Thereafter to don plaids, phillabegs, trews, shoulder belts or bonnets was to become an outlaw and risk imprisonment, even transportation.

But the tartans have proved as indestructible as the clans themselves. Both are still with us. New tartans are being designed and in Edinburgh the Lord Lyon King of Arms — final arbiter in all matters of Scottish heraldry — still gravely hands down judgements on claims to clan chiefships and entitlement to sport given tartans, badges or arms.

◆ C L A N   H I S T O R Y ◆

The Gaelic *Clann*, origin of the modern word clan, simply signifies the children of the family, the kith and kin. This is the key to understanding the unique Scottish clan system, which has survived down through the centuries and whose steadfast bonds, stretching across oceans and continents, still fascinate the world.

The system grew out of the ancient Celtic tribal principles of the kinship of free men with their tribal leader though, as several historians have pointed out, this did not mean it was necessarily a democratic system, since the chiefships were hereditary and regarded with a certain reverence, while there was also a well-defined system of earls, thanes, and freemen.

What membership of the clan has always uniquely offered is a communal pride in the blood-line, a knowledge that since the family itself is noble and brave all of its children can share equally in its glory. This is a pride quite unconnected with social rank, economic power or class status. Rather, it is a high

regard for the achievements of the family group headed by a patriarchal leader-figure to whom his descendants give due respect while feeling able to contribute to the clan's well-being as equals.

The 16th-century French were the "auld allies" of the Scots, to whom they freely offered the right to become naturalized French subjects. With their rigid social rankings, they were fascinated by the mystical powers of the clan system which, they joked derisively, allowed the poorest Scot to claim kinship with Kings. And indeed this was the truth of the system, diametrically opposite to the European feudal structure and its emphasis on private property owned by an overlord with serfs and vassals below him.

The unique clan system has grown out of the Scottish sense of family and racial continuity. It is based on tribal kinship and tribal identification with ancestral lands. A clan's territories have always been the heartland, the homeland of all its children, to be guarded and fought for by all. This love of their land is the pulse-beat of the Scots. "My heart's in the Highlands, my heart is not here" explained both Robert Burns and Walter Scott. This combination of pride of race with pride of soil created a powerful social system, not merely for military purposes but for the welfare of all the clan's kith and kin. The good chief protected his clansmen, putting his patriarchal obligations before his personal rights.

The tribal system was first brought to Scotland by those Irish Celts known as Scots, perhaps having earlier emigrated to Ireland from Spain. A nomadic folk of Indo-Aryan origin, the Celts founded no cities on their way to the fringes of Western Europe. But they carried with them such a wealth of culture

The Battle of Culloden, where Bonnie Prince Charlie failed in his attempt to regain the throne of England and Scotland and the Jacobite cause was lost forever. The battle was fought on 16 April, 1746. This engraving was published in November, 1797.

Roman church, was the soul of the Celtic society while the tribe was its body.

The 9th-century Viking raids, particularly devastating for such intellectual seats of Celtic lore as the monastery of Iona, where much of Western learning was stored in the library, damaged the peaceful Celtic structure and temporarily hindered the growth of the Scottish clan system. Fortunately, one of the few manuscripts to survive, the Book of Kells, was saved from the Vikings by being rowed across the sea to the Columban monastery in Ireland whose name it bears. Some men of learning managed to escape to Europe, leaving Scotland much poorer for their going.

Once the Vikings were finally vanquished in the 13th century, the clan system was able to expand in a medieval Scotland whose central administration was so inefficient that the clan territories became miniature Celtic states, equivalents of today's regional authorities. The chiefs held sway and kept order, at the same time having to take note of their kinsmen's needs and wishes. Strangely, the Lothians, where Edinburgh, Scotland's capital, is located, is the one area of the country that has always been excluded from the clan system. This is probably because when King David I came to the throne in 1124, followed by his Norman friends from England, the first land grants he made to them were in the Lothians.

By the 15th century the clan network was so well established, not only in the Highlands but right down the length of Scotland and into the Lowlands, as far south as Galloway, that it was able to control lawlessness and provide its own forms of justice. Like other Scottish institutions, the laws earned an independent respect (unlike in the rest of Europe, where serfdom enslaved the common people). This integrity, and the spiritual identification of the Scottish clans with the land, meant that the anarchy and distintegration which overwhelmed the Irish tribal system never affected Scotland in the same way.

Though Scottish history may seem to present a picture of clans constantly at each other's throats it was only when two of the mightier and greater clans crossed swords that smaller ones were sucked into the battle and large areas were fought over. Otherwise the system provided a stabilizing structure, natural justice and fair use of the land.

The close Scottish identification with the land has even saved some of the most beautiful scenery in the world from being commercially exploited and ruined, largely because clan chiefs have recognized their obligation to present-day and future generations of kinsmen. The Colquhouns of Luss, for instance, owners of the renowned landscapes around Loch Lomond, have steadfastly refused tempting offers for their land. Unfortunately a new threat lies in the nature of modern global warfare; the Ministry of Defence is thrusting a new road through Glen Fruin, site of the battlefield where hundreds of Colquhouns were massacred by the Macgregors in the 17th century, so that the Trident nuclear submarine base can be constructed on the Clyde. This act of vandalism is deeply opposed by the Colquhoun chief.

The most ruthless attack on the clan system was mounted by the Hanoverian government in revenge for the near-success — almost miraculous in the face of the odds — of the ill-equipped Jacobite army that marched on London, almost putting the King to flight before they halted at Derby. The de-Celticisation of the Highlands began with the 1746 defeat in battle at Culloden of Bonnie Prince Charlie, the Stewart claimant to the thrones of Scotland and England, which his ancestor, James VI of Scotland and I of England, had united in 1603. When the Prince returned to Scotland with a handful of followers and raised his standard at Glenfinnan, the most romantic — and perhaps foolhardy — aspect of the clans' steely mixture of duty and devotion was demonstrated. When he fled, to become once again the "King across the water", the weakest and most destructive element of clan loyalty was revealed, for the clans put

that Gaelic has one of the oldest literatures, and its bards have always had the place of honour at a chief's table.

The clan system also owes much to the hereditary character of the Celtic church, which was established in Scotland by Irish princely missionaries — first St. Ninian, in the 5th century, at Whithorn, in the far South of Scotland; later and more effectively, by St. Columba, who landed on the Hebridean island of Iona in 563. Columba's statesmanship united the Scots against the Picts, earlier inhabitants who had crossed the North Sea to settle on both shores of the Moray Firth, in north-eastern Scotland. In return it was a Scottish nobleman called Patrick who went back over the Irish Sea to become the patron saint of Ireland.

Like all other Scottish institutions the Celtic church had both a tribal and a hereditary structure, with a married priesthood and a lineage of hereditary abbots, perhaps comparable with the Levites of the Old Testament, from whom some of the older Scottish clans can claim descent. It has been said that this form of Christianity, so fundamentally different from that of the their trust not just in weakling princes but also in their all-too fallible chiefs.

What followed was a ruthless, systematic purge of the tribal system and its culture. The initial bloody atrocities of the soldiers, who murdered prisoners and burnt the wounded alive, were followed by a whole series of laws, designed to confiscate the rebel chiefs' estates and handing over their running to bureaucrats, mainly lawyers in Edinburgh. The clansmen were forbidden to wear the kilt or the tartan, to play the bagpipes or carry weapons, and were also banned from becoming factors of the forfeited estates. New roads and bridges, constructed by General Wade, were driven like stakes through the heart of the Highlands so that troops could be positioned in strategic villages, ready to quell the first sign of fresh rebellion. Perhaps just as significant, the powers of the old clan councils and courts were weakened, as the rule of southern law was imposed. Instead of reckoning their wealth in terms of fighting men, even chiefs who kept their lands became impoverished and were forced to begin demanding high rents from their clansmen. Demoralized by their defeat at Culloden, heartsick at the soulless administration imposed on their clan lands, turned almost into slaves by the loss of the friendly warmth of the clan chieftainship structure, the clansmen began to emigrate. These first waves of migrants were to become a 19th-century flood.

First to go were the tacksmen, often younger brothers or cousins of clan chiefs, tenants who had a "tack", or lease, of their land from the chief and who then sublet it to tenants whom in times of danger they could summon to arms. Scotland's loss of what could have become her modern entrepreneurs was America's gain. Often taking some of their clansmen tenants with them, they headed mainly for North Carolina to join those who had fled after Culloden. There they founded new Scottish clan societies and delighted in the freedom to wear their national dress again.

Others joined the Highland regiments which had been formed principally to defuse the martial spirit of the clans as well as to fight against France. When those wars ended in 1763 and the regiments were disbanded, another wave of Scottish settlers headed for the Carolinas.

Meanwhile agricultural changes in the Highlands meant that potatoes were displacing oats as the principal crop, changing from the old runrig system of small arable strips of land to the more minimal acreage, or crofts, needed to grow potatoes, which might even then be further divided to provide a living for sons. At the same time the price of wool rose, making sheep-farming, even on the hilly and stony Highlands, a feasible proposition. Anyone with even a passing interest in Scotland's history knows that it was the introduction of sheep which, symbolically, dealt the final blow to the ancient Highland culture. The Highland Clearances, the eviction of men to make way for animals, put a cruel end to the Highlander's faith in his chief.

The Clearances were a terrible scourge of the Highland people. From 1782 onwards whole boatloads of Scots crossed the Atlantic from their Hebridean or West Highland homes. The migration which had started with a trickle of tacksmen from the mid-1700s was now actively encouraged, even paid for, by clan chiefs from the early 1800s onwards. The clan lands were handed over to sheep — nowhere more brutally than in the Strathnaver glens of the Countess of Sutherland, where fire, dogs and armed men cleared Highlanders from their homes — and bitter memories were carried across the Atlantic.

As Dr. Samuel Johnson wrote after his tour of the Highlands, "there never was any change of national manners so quick, so great and so general as that which has operated in the Highlands by the last conquest and subsequent laws".

Though their lands were turned into sheep farms, deer forests, and grouse moors, often by Lowland or English capitalists, the spirit of the clans was never completely broken. As they fol-

The Battle of Sheriffmuir (1715),
painted by John Wooton. This was
the first Jacobite attempt to regain
the throne, by James, the Old
Pretender to the throne of England
and Scotland, father of Bonnie Prince
Charlie. The outcome of the battle
was indecisive, but James left the
country.

lowed their families into exile in America or Australia, Canada or New Zealand, the clan members carried with them their ancestral pride in their Scottish heritage. Today clan societies thrive all over the world and still recognize their chiefs, some of whom went into exile with them. Some clans have become wealthy enough to repurchase at least some part of their old homelands, and even their castles, the chiefs' seats, to be held irrevocably and forever in trust for the clan.

· T A R T A N S ·

The tartans of Scotland are traditionally unique outward symbols of the ancient clan system that still identifies and bonds Scotsmen and Scotswomen all over the world.

So important was the tartan garb in its identification with Scottish national and tribal pride that the wearing of it was totally banned after the defeat of Bonnie Prince Charlie at Culloden in 1746 as part of an attempt to break up the clan system for ever. Highland dress was completely outlawed by the Hanoverian government in London, which decreed in the 1747 Act for the Abolition and Proscription of Highland Dress that no man or boy within that part of Great Britain called Scotland, other than serving soldiers, should wear the plaid, phillabeg, trews, shoulder belts or any other item of Highland dress. No tartan or particoloured plaid was to be used, and anyone found wearing Highland dress was to be imprisoned for six months on a first offence. Those convicted a second time were liable to be transported "to any of His Majesty's plantations beyond the seas, there to remain for a space of seven years".

Those who disobeyed this oppressive law were treated as outlaws. In 1748, the Hanoverian troops who roamed the Highlands crushing the rebellious Jacobite clans were ordered to kill on the spot any men wearing Highland dress. Even in the Lowland capital of Edinburgh a woman was arrested for wearing a tartan-patterned dress. Only men serving in Highland regiments were allowed their tartan kilts.

The raising of the Highland regiments, starting with the most famous of them all, the Black Watch, was another way of controlling the hostile Scots, by enrolling them in the British army. The clans were at their lowest ebb in history, and for many Highlanders the only hope of earning a living lay in fighting foreign wars. Frasers, Macdonalds, Camerons, Macleans and Macphersons, among other Jacobite supporters, were enrolled by their chiefs. But, as always, they insisted on wearing their clan tartans into battle, whether fighting in Europe or in the American War of Independence.

When Fraser's Highlanders, the old 78th, landed in America the kilt was considered unsuitable for the severe winters and hot summers, but both officers and soldiers vehemently refused to wear anything else. Soon, as the migrant Scots settlers tasted the freedom of being able to wear once again their traditional dress, a great demand for tartan arose in the New World.

The military exemption to the ban on wearing the kilt was the saving of the tartan. But in 1782, when after 35 years the ban was finally lifted, the old Highland practice of isolated village weavers first dyeing and then turning out the individual clan setts, or patterns, had been more or less destroyed. The setts, carefully counted out in their intricate colour combinations, had in some cases been forgotten, and much confusion arose over which were the authentic clan tartans.

The Highland Society of London, which had been set up in 1778 for the express purpose of restoring Highland dress and preserving Gaelic culture and music, turned its attention to bringing back the kilt. Its president was General Fraser of Lovat, and among its members were Lord Macdonald, the Earl of Seaforth, Lord Gordon, Colonel Macpherson of Cluny and Cameron of Erracht. In 1782 the Society asked another parlia-

Prince Charles Edward ("Bonnie Prince Charlie") landing on Eriskay in the Outer Hebrides on his return to Scotland on 23 April, 1745. Painting by unknown artist of the French School, c.1800.

mentary member, the Marquis of Graham (later the Duke of Montrose), to put forward a Bill that would repeal the earlier Act. In his successful pleadings Lord Graham claimed that bringing back Highland dress would "keep a useful body of subjects on this side of the Atlantic".

Some 30 years later the Society began collecting authentic tartans, writing to clan chiefs and heads of families and asking for samples of their tartans to save the old patterns from being irrevocably lost. The Society's collection of more than 300 pieces of tartan has now been placed in the Royal Museum of Scotland and is the subject of computer analysis by researchers at the Scottish College of Textiles in the Borders.

But the great boost for tartan's reinstatement came in 1822, from Sir Walter Scott, who had popularized so many of the Highland legends in his romantic novels. Now he energetically stage-managed the visit of George IV to Edinburgh, the first to the Scottish capital by a Hanoverian monarch. All the clan chiefs were summoned to meet the King, and everyone, from the grossly overweight King himself to the Lord Mayor of London and the clan chiefs, parading in the Lowlands, was arrayed in Highland dress, making a superb display of the tartan.

Another monarch, Queen Victoria, completed the reinstatement of the tartan by her enthusiam for all things Scottish, which extended to draping her Scottish home, Balmoral Castle, in all kinds of tartan hangings and having her own Balmoral tartan woven. From then on tartans were universally popular, not only in Scotland but throughout Europe, and remained so into the 20th century, both as multi-coloured cloths and as the traditional Scottish dress of the kilt. As Sir Walter Scott truly remarked, "the kilt is an ancient dress, a martial dress and a becoming dress".

The origins of tartan itself are mysteriously obscure. The Irish Celts, who later crossed the Irish Sea to settle in Scotland, probably wore the first form of the kilt, modelled on the Roman tunic. In Gaelic this was known as *Leine-chroich*, the word for a shirt that stopped short just above the knee, usually made of linen and dyed saffron yellow, still the colour of Irish kilts today. To display rank the Irish marked their shirts with stripes, the King himself having seven stripes and the next below him, the

Blair Castle, at Blair Atholl near
Pitlochry in the southern Highlands,
ancestral home of the Murray family.
Queen Victoria stayed at the castle
when she visited Scotland.

The West Point tartan, designed by
Kinloch Anderson Ltd. to be worn by
students at the military academy at
West Point, N.Y.

man of learning, having six. The Hebridean Scots probably wore this loose garment buckled at the waist. In 1093, a Norseman, Magnus Barefoot, introduced the garb into Norway on his return from voyaging round the Western Isles. A sculptured stone in Ross-shire, dating from the 7th century, shows a Highlander wearing a kilt and a sporran.

It has also been conjectured that the word tartan comes from the Old French *tiretaine*, meaning merely a cloth made of mixed wool and cotton. Yet by the mid-16th century French soldiers serving in Scotland were remarking upon the Highlanders who were naked but for their stained or saffron-dyed shirts and their other covering made of wool in various colours. George Buchanan, the Scots historian and tutor — first of Mary, Queen of Scots and then of her son, James VI & I — described in 1582 how the Highlanders delighted in variegated garments, favouring purples and blues. But darker shades were becoming more customary as camouflage to conceal the wearers in the heather when, wrapped in their tartans, they lay down to sleep out of doors, even in severe storms. Still earlier, the father of Mary Queen of Scots, James V, had worn a form of Highland dress consisting of tartan trews (trousers) and a long shirt. Their cost is recorded in the Court accounts.

Tartan is a word unknown to the Highlanders. The Gaelic version is *breacan*, which means chequered. *Breacan-feile* means "the belted plaid", the first unsewn combination of the kilt and the plaid, made of 12 ells (15 yds/15 m) of tartan, the lower part forming the kilt. "Plaid" is often used, particularly by Americans, to refer to tartans. But the plaid was the other half of this continuous garment, formed from the rest of the fabric and flung loosely over the shoulder, where it was pinned with a brooch (jewelled pin), and left to hang down the back. This left the arms free for fighting, while at the same time providing enough loose fabric to wrap round the body in bad weather, or at night to form a primitive sleeping-bag. The *feileadh-beag*, or in its anglicized form, phillabeg (spelt also fillabeg), means "the little kilt", which took only half the amount of tartan cloth and was the precursor of the modern kilt. Dispensing with the loose, over-the-shoulder plaid, the phillabeg was originally just loosely gathered and held round the waist with a strap, though some of the cloth probably protruded above the strap. The flat, stitched-down pleating seen in the modern kilt may have been invented by regimental tailors trying to make the Highland regiments, raised in the 18th century, look more spick and span. By the 17th century the phillabeg was much more commonplace than the *breacan-feile*, as were some of the other modern accoutrements of Highland dress, such as the sporran, or purse — which evolved from the drawstring bag that travellers used to carry — as well as the chequered hose and the brogues. "Trews", from the Gaelic *triubhes*, were tartan trousers, cut crossways and worn generally by the chiefs and gentlemen. The setts (patterns) of the tartan in the trews were generally smaller than those of the kilt.

By the time of the 1745 Jacobite rebellion clan chiefs were wearing a full-trimmed bonnet, tartan jacket, vest, kilt and cross-belt, a tartan belted plaid, or cloak, hose, brogues, a silver-mounted purse, or sporran, and a belt. By then the clans also had their own identifying tartans, easily distinguishable on the battlefield, though these were still not so formalized as they became in the later 19th and 20th centuries. Initially, clans had identified themselves by wearing plants as badges. The different tartan patterns became a more uniform method of identification only around the late 17th and early 18th centuries. The weaving of tartans was very much a local craft industry, the vegetable dyes being made from local lichens, mosses and other plants and the women keeping a careful count, sometimes on rods, of the layout of checks and stripes in the various patterns. The destruction of the clan system and the

The Macdonald Boys, Sir James and Sir Alex by an unknown artist. The picture is believed to have been painted c.1750, when the wearing of tartans was still banned. The remoteness of the MacDonald home may have enabled them to break the law. The boys are wearing between them four different MacDonald tartans.

banning of Highland dress led also to the disruption of this Highland crofting industry. Later the Victorian fad for wearing tartan created a whole new machine-made tartan industry in the Lowlands.

Research into the very complex subject of the authenticity and age of tartans — more than 1,000 are now recorded — is currently being scientifically conducted.

Tartan is very much alive and well in Scotland today, with new patterns being constantly added to the time-honoured clan setts. The Edinburgh firm of Kinloch Anderson is the proud holder of three royal warrants as kilt-makers to the Queen, the Duke of Edinburgh and the Prince of Wales, and is constantly being asked to help undertake genealogical research and to register new tartans. The United States military academy at West Point and British Caledonian Airways, whose air hostesses wear tartan kilts, are just two organizations which have been awarded the special privilege of having their own individual tartans. West Point's tartan, worn by its military band, has been granted and registered by the Lord Lyon, the Scottish King of Arms, who is the final arbiter on all matters pertaining to the clans and their arms, accoutrements and Highland dress. Both of these tartans were designed by Kinloch Anderson, in consultation with the eventual wearers and with the Lord Lyon.

The Lord Lyon has powers to bring to his court — which has full legal status under Scottish law, unlike England's Royal College of Heralds — all those who sport clan badges, arms and tartans without right or permission. Individuals wishing to have tartans registered can apply to the Lord Lyon, whose office is in Edinburgh's Register House, where all the Scottish births, deaths and marriages are registered.

One who did so is the London-based Scottish author, Willy Newlands, whose family come from Banffshire and were falconers to James IV in the 1490s. He started by researching into his family history and came across an old, hand-woven piece of tartan which had become part of a cushion cover. He wrote to the Scottish Tartan Society, who put him in touch with an Inverness-shire tartan specialist. Unfortunately the tartan remnant was too small to show the full sett, but the expert was able to extend the pattern, which has now been registered as both the Newlands and the Scottish falconers' tartan.

Mr Newlands reckons that having his arms and his tartan registered with the Lord Lyon has cost him some £700, while getting his own tartan woven will cost about £15-20 per yard, the minimum order being 60 yards at a time. But Willy Newlands hopes that the rest of his family will help out by buying lengths of the dark green and blue Newlands tartan, rather similar to that of Cameron of Erracht, with its four red cross-stripes. He says, anyway, that despite the cost it has all been a fascinating and worthwhile exercise that will also allow his wife, Dorothy Walker-Newlands, to wear with pride a sash of the family tartan.

His enjoyable experience, combining family lore and tradition with the legal heraldry of Scotland — to this day still called upon to decide the rightful clan chiefs — is an example of the constant development of tartan. This cloth of the clans, developing naturally out of the mists and mountains and muted natural colours of a most beautiful country and the mystical devotion of its people to an ancient culture, has survived the repression of its very use and the fickle flattery of becoming high fashion. Though kilts and tartans have been copied, changed and adapted by dress designers in many countries, from Japan to France, its basic significance, its emotional role in Scotland's long history as a nation, remains undiminished.

Portrait of General Douglas MacArthur in needlepoint, from the MacArthur Memorial in Norfolk, Virginia.

The clans

and their
tartans

Those two most Scottish of names, Anderson (the Lowland form) and MacAndrew (the Highland version), both mean son of Andrew, the patron saint of Scotland. They are well-represented in American history since one of the clan, Adam Anderson, was a founder of the colony of Georgia in 1732 and, with his fellow Scots, defended the settlement against the Spaniards from the fort they built and named St. Andrews. The Gaelic form of the name is Gillanders, literally, the servant or ghillie of St. Andrew.

The MacAndrews are part of that powerful Confederation of Highland clans, the clan Chattan. The fighting qualities of one of these Highlanders, known in Gaelic as Iain Beg MacAindra, was renowned throughout 17th-century Badenoch, where he once killed most of a party of cattle raiders single-handed.

The Lowland Andersons have a more distinguished record as men of science. Alexander Anderson's early 17th century treatises on geometry and algebra gained European recognition. James Gregory, the inventor of the reflecting telescope, was a member of the same family through the female line. In 1773, James Anderson, a farmer's son from Midlothian, wrote the entry on monsoons for the first edition of the *Encyclopaedia Britannica*, forecasting the discoveries to be made by Captain Cook.

An even greater contribution to Scotland's great academic traditions was made by John Anderson (1726-1796), Professor of Natural Philosophy at Glasgow University, who, as well as inventing a way to reduce the recoil in a gun, helped to found one of Scotland's eight universities. On his death, he bequeathed all his possessions to inaugurate the Anderson Institute, now Strathclyde University, Glasgow's second university.

The 20th century has produced its share of eminent Andersons. Edinburgh-born John Anderson, a member of Churchill's war-time cabinet who later became Viscount Waverley, commissioned the domestic air-raid shelters which were built in the back-gardens of British homes during World War II and became known as Anderson shelters.

The clan's motto is "Stand Sure" and its badge an oak tree.

TARTAN Those entitled to wear the Anderson tartan include the family of Ross, since the Highland MacAndrews are thought to be an offshoot of the Clan Andreas (Ross), and the Mackintoshes, leaders of the Clan Chattan.

The numerous Armstrong clan first won dubious fame as Border *reivers*, those cattle raiders whose lawless ways kept the wild uplands between Scotland and England, where the boundaries were not settled until 1237, in constant turmoil for several centuries after that. Modern descendants of those bold "moss-troopers" (another name for the Border cattle *reivers* (robbers) have been just as daring and adventurous. An Armstrong explored the North-West passage and named an island in the Canadian Arctic and an American Armstrong took that momentous "great step for mankind" on the moon. The Armstrongs can (if they wish) also claim an American President; Nixon is a sept name of the clan.

Brave beginnings are said to be the origin of this clan's name, honourably won on the battlefield. Legend has its progenitor as a King's armour bearer — possibly named Fairbairn — who saved his master when he was dismounted by snatching him up onto his own horse through the strength of his arm. Hence the name, granted by the King, along with lands in Liddesdale in the Borders. From here the clan expanded into Annandale and Eskdale.

The swaggering story of Johnnie Armstrong of Gilnockie, who in 1529 commanded 3,000 men and was the virtual king of the Borders is told in one of the most splendid of the Border ballads. Unarmed, he rode out merrily to meet King James V, prepared to entertain him right royally at his keep. But the King had other plans for his lawless subject. He and his men were surrounded and Johnnie, despite pleading for his life, was summarily hanged from the nearest tree. The ruins of Gilnockie tower can still be seen beside the beautiful banks of the River Esk.

This rough justice brought retribution to the King. When Henry VIII invaded Scotland in 1542 the Borderers surrendered tamely at the battle of Solway Moss rather than fight for the King who had executed Johnnie Armstrong. At the beginning of the 17th century, in the final subjugation of the Borders, many leading Armstrongs were executed and their strongholds razed to the ground until hardly any lands were left to them.

The clan motto is *Invictus Maneo* — "I remain unvanquished", and its badge is a strong right arm.

TARTAN Though the clan has no Highland associations it does have this tartan, predominantly dark green, blue, and black with thin red stripes. Those septs entitled to wear it include Crosier, Fairbairn, Grozier and Nixon.

The Bairds are another clan whose origins are attributed to saving a King, this time King William the Lion, who was in danger of being killed by a wild boar. In grateful thanks the King presented lands to this brave Baird.

The first land charter, recorded in the 13th century, mentions Richard Baird of Meikle and Little Kyp in Lanarkshire, central Scotland. Later the Bairds spread to Banffshire in the North-east and then to Auchmeddan, Aberdeenshire. Here they grew in importance, and provided a long line of Aberdeenshire sheriffs, and, in the 17th century, a law lord of the Court of Session.

In the next century, Sir David Baird was a famous General, fighting all over the world, first in India, then, in 1807, gaining renown by capturing the Cape of Good Hope in South Africa from the Dutch, and finally taking command at Corunna in Spain after Sir John Moore was killed.

The best-known Baird of the 20th century is John Logie Baird, the minister's son from Helensburgh, near Glasgow, who invented television in 1926.

The clan motto is *Dominus fecit* — "The Lord made" — and its badge is an eagle's head.

TARTAN This family tartan, a mixture of greens and blacks with broad purple stripes, bears some resemblance in its setting to that of the Gordons.

The Barclays arrived in Scotland from either Gloucestershire or Somersetshire in England, and may have originally have been Normans who, like the English Berkeleys, crossed the Channel with William the Conqueror.

Certainly, by 1165, Sir Walter de Berkeley of Gartly was Lord Chamberlain of Scotland, and in the next century there were numerous members of the family in Kincardineshire and the East of Scotland.

Until 1456 the chieftaincy passed down directly from Sir Walter de Berkeley, until it went through a female into the Towie-Barclay branch, descendants of Sir Walter's brother, Alexander, whose son had been the first to spell the name "Barclay".

The chief of the Towie Barclay line — the main branch of the clan — Peter Barclay, who lives at 137 Mill Road, Mile End, Colchester in Essex, inerited the title from his American cousin in 1967. Towie Barclay estate was sold off in the 18th century, but the great keep of Towie Barclay, near Turiff, Banffshire, has been restored and made into his family home by a Canadian, Marc Ellington. The Towie Barclay line also produced a Russian Field Marshal, Prince Barclay de Tolly, who commanded the army which defeated Napoleon in 1812.

The descendant of another line of Barclays whose lands were at Urie, near Stonehaven, Kincardineshire, was Robert Barclay, who became a Quaker and a friend of William Penn. Together they travelled throughout Europe, spreading the Quaker message.

The Barclay clan motto is *Aut augere aut mori* — "Either action or death" — and its badge a hand holding aloft a dagger.

TARTAN The vivid Barclay dress tartan is bright yellow with thick black and thin white stripes.

The Barclay hunting tartan has the same pattern as the dress tartan, but on a green ground.

Lord Kilmarnock, who lives in Malaga, Spain, is chief of the clan Boyd, whose name is thought to derive from *Bod*, the Gaelic for Bute, the beautiful island in the Firth of Clyde. The first to take this island's name were Normans who had travelled there, probably with the de Moreville family from England. Later, the clan spread into south-west Scotland, where Boyd is the name of a town in Ayrshire.

The first Lord Boyd, son of Sir Thomas Boyd of Kilmarnock, seized the Scottish throne by kidnapping the young James III, whose tutor in knightly ways he was. Fortunately, he proved to be a good and able ruler, and his royal connections were strengthened when, in 1467, his son, Thomas, married the King's sister, Mary, and was made Earl of Arran, taking his name from the neighbouring island to Bute.

In 1469, the Earl went to Norway to arrange his brother-in-law's marriage to the Norwegian princess, Christian, whose dowry brought the Northern Isles of Orkney and Shetland to the Scottish Crown. But before the Norwegian princess could arrive in Scotland, the all-powerful Boyds were toppled by their rivals. The Earl of Arran was saved only by his wife sailing out to his ship to warn him, and he fled to the Low Countries where he died. His widow, the Princess Mary, was then forced to marry Lord Hamilton, who took the title of Arran and thus became next in line to the throne.

The title was restored to the Boyds in 1536 and in 1661 the 10th Lord Boyd was made the Earl of Kilmarnock by Charles II. At Culloden the 4th Earl commanded the cavalry of Bonnie Prince Charlie. He was beheaded on London's Tower Hill, and the title forfeited.

However, the executed Earl's second son inherited another title through a great-aunt, that of the Earl of Erroll, and adopted the surname of Hay. A century later, the Earldom of Kilmarnock was acquired by the Hays. In 1941, Kilmarnock became a separate title once again when the 22nd Earl of Erroll died. While his daughter succeeded him as chief of Clan Hay and Countess of Erroll, his brother became the 6th Lord Kilmarnock and chief of Clan Boyd. The present chief, the 7th Lord Kilmarnock, has written several travel guides to Spain, where he now lives.

TARTAN The clan's royal links are recalled in their tartan, which is very similar to that of the Royal Stewart tartan.

Ninian Brodie of Brodie, the 25th chief of this clan, still lives in Brodie castle, Morayshire, parts of which date back to the 16th century. Nowadays the castle is open to all visitors since the chief, in 1979, handed it over into the safe-keeping of the National Trust for Scotland. As the Trust points out, the Castle's collection of fine paintings, French and English furniture and Chinese porcelain is probably unique in Scotland because of the long, unbroken continuity of the Brodie family history with its estates.

The Brodies are, in fact, one of the original tribes of Morayshire, holding their lands almost beyond human memory. Unfortunately all the ancient family charters were lost when Brodie House was captured by the Gordons, but there was a Thane (a Scottish baron) of Brodie in the 13th century, and King Robert the Bruce gave Michael Brodie of Brodie a charter for his lands in 1311, making the old Celtic thanage into a barony. This proves that the Brodies were no newcomers but ancient aristocrats, possibly even of the royal line, from the time of Macbeth's kingdom, and even earlier Pictish kings. The "blasted heath" where Macbeth supposedly met the witches is not far from the castle.

Though little written evidence of the early family history survives, one remarkable document was discovered at Brodie, in 1972, in a pigeon loft. This was a vellum pontifical, a bishop's office-book, dating from the year 1000. Six generations later, Alexander Brodie of Brodie was so fanatically Presbyterian that he mutilated the carvings and destroyed the religious paintings in Elgin Cathedral. His diary, covering the times of Cromwell and the restoration of Charles II, has been published. Generally though, the Brodies took little part in affairs of state, and so managed to keep their castle intact while others were losing all their possessions.

The clan motto is "Unite" and the badge is a hand holding a sheaf of arrows.

Septs of the clan include such other forms of the name as Brody, Bryde and Brydie.

TARTAN There are three Brodie tartans, the dress and the hunting and the red. The dress tartan, shown here, is older than the hunting tartan, which includes blue and green.

In Scotland's halls of fame, no name is more revered than that of Bruce. Robert the Bruce was Scotland's premier freedom fighter, the brave leader who fought to throw off English domination in the 14th century, inspired, so the story goes, by the tireless example of a spider weaving its web. Resounding down through the centuries comes the thundering triumph of his victory against a much mightier English army, led by Edward II, at Bannockburn in 1314, a victory recalled in Burns' song, "Scots Wha' Hae", which could easily be Scotland's national anthem.

"Scots wha hae wi' Wallace bled, Scots wham Bruce has aften led,
Welcome to your gorie bed, or to victorie!
Now's the day and now's the hour, see the front of battle lour;
See approach proud Edward's power, chains and slaverie."

Like the American Declaration of Independence, another magnificently phrased affirmation of nationhood, Scotland's Declaration of Arbroath, was signed by the Scottish nobles in 1320 while Bruce was King of Scotland.

"For as long as one hundred of us shall remain alive we shall never in any wise consent to submit to the rule of the English, for it is not for glory we fight, for riches or for honours, but for freedom alone, which no good man loses but with his life".

In this century the present heads of the clan Bruce, the Earls of Elgin, helped raise funds to preserve Scotland's most historic site, the battlefield of Bannockburn. A statue of Robert Bruce now dominates the site near Stirling, where the National Trust for Scotland's Heritage Centre tells the tale of Bruce and his battle.

The original Bruces were Normans, with a castle at Brix. They accompanied William the Conqueror to England in 1066. They travelled to Scotland in the 12th century with David I when he became King and were rewarded with lands in Annandale, Dumfriesshire. In the 13th century, they married into the royal house and in 1238 the sixth Robert the Bruce of Annandale, the King having no heir, was named next in line to the Scottish throne. His grandson, the freedom fighter, was finally crowned in 1306 after the Scottish King, John Balliol, had been deposed by the English.

The reign of Robert the Bruce brought about the rise of newly-powerful Scottish families, who had supported him and were rewarded with lands; the fortunes of others, who had been on the wrong side, declined. Robert the Bruce's own line ended with the death of his son, King David II, in 1371.

David II had given the barony of Clackmannan to his "cousin" Robert Bruce, and this family continued living there until their line died out in 1791. King Robert the Bruce's great two-handed sword was passed on to another Bruce, the Earl of Elgin, in whose possession it still remains at the family home of Broomhall, Fife.

The Elgins have another claim to fame: it was the 7th Earl who bought the marbles of the Greek Parthenon and presented them to the British Museum in 1816. They are now known as the Elgin marbles. The charming 16th-century palace of another Bruce, the wealthy, coal-mining Laird of Culross in Fife, Sir George Bruce, was the first purchase ever made by the fledgling National Trust for Scotland in the 1930s, and is now the centrepiece of this restored 16th-century coastal village.

The clan motto is *Fuimus* — "We have been" — and the badge depicts a lion.

TARTAN The Bruce tartan has a red background with green checks and alternate yellow and white stripes. Septs include Carlyle, Carruthers, Crosbie, Randolph and Stenhouse.

The Buchanan clan presently has no chief. However, the Buchanans probably have the oldest established clan society in Scotland, owning the clan's most precious possession, its heartland, from which it takes its war-cry. That is the tiny island, measuring just half a mile in length, of Clar Innis or Clarinch on Loch Lomond, where in 1225 the family is first recorded. That was when the island was given to Sir Anselan or Absalon of Buchanan, said to be a son of Macbeth. But in Gaelic *Buth Chanai* means the house (or seat) of the canon, which may denote that the Buchanans have ecclesiastical origins, and are hereditary clerics of the Celtic church. Another theory is that the Buchanans descend from the son of a King of Ulster, Anselan o'Kyan, who landed in Argyll at the beginning of the 11th century.

Certainly, the Buchanans were early members of the Scottish intelligentsia, with a keen interest in religion down the centuries. The most famous intellectual was the 16th-century poet, George Buchanan, renowned in Europe as a Latin scholar, who was born at Killearn, Stirlingshire. Although he became converted to Calvinism, he was tutor first to Mary Queen of Scots, and then, although he cruelly libelled her, to her son, James VI & I, who was dubbed "the wisest fool in Christendom". Another Scottish Calvinist, James Buchanan, settled first in Donegal and then went to America, where his son, also called James Buchanan, became the 15th President.

The Buchanan lands, lying to the east of Loch Lomond, remained in the family for almost seven centuries, until they were sold in 1682 to the Marquess of Montrose, on the death of John, the 22nd laird. Despite the fact that there were many cadet branches — Leny, Carbeth, Drumakill, Arnprior, Spittal and Auchmar — the clan thereafter became dispersed.

In 1723, William Buchanan of Auchmar published a book about the origins of the clan and family Buchanan. Two years later the Buchanan Society, a charitable organisation founded to help needy clansfolk and to educate boys, was set up in Glasgow. More than 200 years later, a wealthy clansman bequeathed the island of Clarinch to the Society as an animal and bird sanctuary.

The clan motto is *Clarior hinc Honos* — "Brighter hence the honour" — and its crest is a hand holding a tasselled cap.

TARTAN The gaily checked red, yellow and green Buchanan old sett tartan is one of the most popularly worn. Even the Buchanan hunting tartan is more colourful than the sombre greens used by other clans.

The Camerons, amongst the most ancient of Highland clans, have held their wild Lochaber lands in Inverness-shire by dint of fighting tenacity down the centuries. The present chief, Sir Donald Cameron of Lochiel, 26th in the direct line and bearer of one of the most romantic Jacobite names, still lives in the clan seat of Achnacarry, near Spean Bridge, where the Commandos trained during World War II.

The clan name is said to come from the Gaelic *Cam-shron*, meaning "the crooked nose", possibly that of an early chief. The surname Cambron is recorded in Lochaber in the 13th century, and the clan, described as "fiercer than fierceness itself" in the 17th century, expanded into the hills around Loch Lochy, Loch Arkaig and Loch Eil. The Camerons had to be fiercely courageous to keep their lands — the Cameron war-cry is "Sons of the hounds come here and get flesh" — as they had no legal title to them until Ewen, the 13th chief adopted the title of Cameron of Lochiel in 1528 when he was granted the barony.

Always on the side of the Stewart kings, the 17th chief, Sir Ewen, was one of the few Highland chiefs whom Cromwell failed to subdue. His grandson, Donald, is forever revered to as "the gentle LLochiel", the man of peace who became the hero of the 1745 rebellion. He initially advised Bonnie Prince Charlie to return to France, but when his advice was unheeded, Lochiel mustered 700 of his clansmen at Glenfinnan, making the rising possible. Wounded in both legs at Culloden, Lochiel was hidden in the hills before escaping with the Prince to France. His brother, Dr. Archibald Cameron, was the last Jacobite to be hung, drawn and quartered.

Sadly, 19th-century chiefs betrayed their clansmen by evicting them so that more money could be raised from their lands to rebuild Achnacarry Castle, destroyed by the Hanoverian troops. Many Camerons joined the Highland regiments after the '45, and some fought in the American wars, like Alan Cameron of Erracht, who became a prisoner of the American rebels from 1775 to 1778. Later, in 1793, he raised the 79th Highlanders, which became the Queen's Own Cameron Highlanders.

The clan motto is "Unite" and its badge a sheaf of five arrows.

TARTAN There are three Cameron tartans in general use. This one, the Cameron of Lochiel, has a red background but lacks the yellow stripe used in the green and red general Cameron tartan. The third is the Erracht or Cameron Highlanders' tartan, devised by its founder's mother, as a blend of the Macdonald and Cameron tartans. The Cameron clan has a large number of septs.

The Duke of Argyll, one of the six Scottish Dukes with his seat at Inveraray Castle, Argyllshire, is chief of the clan Campbell, which is said to have twelve and a half million world-wide. The present 12th Duke of Argyll is also Hereditary Master of the Queen's Household in Scotland, Keeper of the Great Seal of Scotland, Keeper of Dunoon, Carrick, Dunstaffnage and Tarbert Castles and, for good measure, Admiral of the Western Isles.

The string of titles indicates the importance of the clan Campbell, a name to be conjured with down the centuries. Traditionally, it is known as the clan Diarmid, after the Ossianic hero, Diarmid O'Duine, with whom the wife of Fingal fell in love. In Gaelic *Cam Beul* means "crooked mouth". The clan was already prominent in Dalriada, the earliest Scottish kingdom.

Its power base was strengthened when Sir Colin Campbell of Loch Awe and his two sons supported Robert the Bruce and, as well as receiving grants of land and guardianship of castles, the King's sister married into the clan, a royal liaison which was to be repeated five centuries later when the 9th Duke of Argyll wed Princess Louise, Queen Victoria's daughter. It is from this same Sir Colin that the chiefs take their ancestral Gaelic title of *Mac Cailein Mor* — "great son of Colin". The ruins of his stronghold can still be seen on an island in the Loch under the peaks of Cruachan, the hill which gave the clan its war-cry.

In 1474, Colin, the first Earl of Argyll, founded the town of Inverary, at the head of Loch Fyne, which has been the clan's headquarters ever since. From here, the rise and rise to power of the Campbells continued. They helped the crown to destroy the mighty Lord of the Isles, took over Macdonald lands in Knapdale and Kintyre, then swallowed up the vast Maclean territories in Morvern and the islands of Mull, Tiree and Coll. But their 16th-century persecution of other Highland clans like the Macgregors and the Donalds gave them a reputation for being unscrupulous. But they were less cunning in the 17th century. During that period's civil wars they twice picked the wrong side, resulting in the execution of both the 1st Marquess of Argyll and his son for treason.

More pragmatically, the Campbells, having been granted a dukedom in 1701, fought for the Hanoverian government during the Jacobite risings and were, by 1745, the richest and most powerful clan in Scotland, able to raise over 3,000 men on their own lands, while the next most powerful branch, the Campbells of Breadalbane, could call up another 1,000. It was the Breadalbane Campbells who were involved in 1692 in the massacre of the Macdonalds of Glencoe, through their cadet branch of Glenlyon.

So powerful once was this line, descended from Sir Colin Campbell of Glenorchy, and made first Earls and, then in 1831, Marquesses of Breadalbane, that its history is worth recording separately from that of the House of Argyll. Breadalbane owned vast estates in Perthshire and Argyllshire. Queen Victoria and Prince Albert were royally entertained in 1842 by the second Marquess at his great Taymouth castle with the Breadalbane Highlanders lined up, wearing the Breadalbane tartan. Yet within the last 100 years the line has died out three times, and the castle and most of the estates have been sold.

Another great Campbell house is that of Cawdor, near Nairn, founded by the kidnapping in 1494 of Muriel, baby daughter of the Thane of Cawdor. Archibald, the 2nd Earl of Argyll, and Justice-General, had the child made his ward and a force of Campbells carried her off to Inverary where eventually she married his third son. She returned with him to Cawdor Castle, which is said to have been built on the spot where a donkey, let loose by Lord Cawdor, stopped under a hawthorn tree. The Earls of Cawdor still live in the 16th-century castle, which is now open to the public, and the hawthorn tree, on which the fortunes of the family are said to depend, still flourishes in the castle's vaults.

The Campbells have helped to safeguard Scotland's heritage. In 1899 the 8th Duke of Argyll gave the Abbey of Iona, the island off Mull from which St. Columba spread Christianity to the nation, and its historic sites were put in the care of trustees on condition that it was reroofed and restored for worship. A marble monument to the Duke and his wife stands inside the now completely restored abbey. Dr. John Lorne Campbell, the writer and collector of Scottish songs and stories, recently gave Canna, the most westerly of the small isles of the Inner Hebrides, along with his magnificent Celtic library, to the National Trust for Scotland.

The Campbell motto is *Ne obliviscaris* — "Forget not" — and the badge is a boar's head.

TARTAN There are various Campbell tartans, but the best known and most widely used is this one, the Campbell of Argyll or Campbell of Lochawe, said to be the oldest and based on the Black Watch tartan with alternate yellow and white lines. The Breadalbane Campbell tartan is similar, but lacks white lines. The Campbell of Cawdor incorporates a red stripe.

On both sides of the Atlantic the name Carnegie immediately recalls the American dream, that of the poor Scots immigrant who made a fortune to become one of the wealthiest men in the world. Ironmaster Andrew Carnegie, son of a Dunfermline linen weaver who emigrated to Pennsylvania in the 1840s, never forgot his native kith and kin, and gave away much of his fortune to found libraries throughout Scotland and provide educational scholarships. He also rebuilt Skibo Castle in Sutherland as his Scottish home.

The name Carnegie first appears in Scottish records in the 13th century in connection with the abbeys of Arbroath and Balmerino, though it comes from the lands of Carmyllie in south-east Angus. These lands were granted to John de Carnegie in 1358, and later acquired by the Carnegies of Kinnaird, near Brechin. In 1633 David, 8th of Kinnaird, became Earl of Southesk, and his brother John was also given an Earldom, that of Northesk (the North and South Esk rivers bisect the county of Angus, both flowing into the North Sea at Montrose).

The Carnegies were always loyal to the Stewart kings, and James Carnegie, of a cadet branch of Northesk, was private secretary to Bonnie Prince Charlie. The 5th Earl of Southesk's title was forfeited after the '45 rising, not to be restored until the 19th century.

The present head of the Carnegies, the 11th Earl of Southesk, still lives at the clan seat in Angus, Kinnaird Castle, Brechin. His son and heir by his first marriage to Princess Maud, granddaughter of Edward VII, inherited the title of Duke of Fife from an aunt and is a second cousin of the Queen. The Duke's heir is the Earl of Macduff.

The clan motto is "Dread God" and its badge a winged thunderbolt.

TARTAN The Carnegie tartan is a variant of the MacDonell of Glengarry, said to have been adopted by Lord Southesk in Jacobite times, when he and Glengarry were side by side. The only variation, replacing a yellow stripe for a white one, may have happened later. It is a family tartan only.

The head of the Chisholm clan is called "The Chisholm" possibly because the name is of Norman origin, originally spelt *De Cheseholm* and first found in the barony of Chieseholme in Roxburghshire. This line survived, latterly as Scott-Chisholme, until the end of the 19th century, when the last Border chief, Colonel John Chisholm, was killed in a charge at Elandslaagte in South Africa.

Originally from the Borders, the family moved north, and by 1359 Sir Robert de Chisholme was Constable of Urquhart Castle on Loch Ness, guarding the vital pass to the Western Highlands. His son, Alexander, married the heiress to the lands of Erchless and Comer, and their son, Thomas, became the first Chisholm chief of the clan, which had the lands of Strathglass and Glen Cannich for the next four centuries. The Chisholms were divided during the Jacobite risings, with the chief's two elder sons fighting for the Hanoverians, whilst the youngest led his clansmen, 30 of whom were killed, at Culloden. Despite this political division, Bonnie Prince Charlie found refuge in Strathglass and three of the seven Glenmoriston men who led him to safety were Chisholms.

In the 18th century the clan began to break up. Many members were forced to emigrate to America because of shortage of land and others were evicted. Ruaridh, the 22nd chief, demanded enormous increases in rent, and although his son Alexander who became the 23rd chief in 1785, resisted the land speculators and offered longer leases to his tenants, the next chief, William, his half-brother, proved most ruthless of all. To make way for sheep he evicted so many tenants that the once populous glens of Cannich and Strathglass became desolate and a Gaelic bard wrote that "the abode of the warriors has withered away. The son of the Lowlander is in your place."

In 1887, Roderick, the chief, died without an heir and after the estates had passed through the female line, they were eventually sold, including the picturesque clan seat of Erchless Castle, Strathglass.

The clan headquarters are at Cnoc-an-Fhurain, Barcaldine, Argyllshire, while the present chief of the Chisholm clan lives at Silver Willows Farm, Beck Row, Bury St Edmunds in Suffolk.

The clan motto is *Feros ferio* — "I am fierce with the fierce" — and its crest is a hand holding aloft a boar's head on the point of a dagger.

TARTAN There are two versions of the Chisholm tartan. This one is a version of the Atholl Stewart; the other is based on the Mackintosh.

The Clan of the Cats, as the clan Chattan is sometimes called from its badge of a wild cat and its motto, is a confederation of tribes, an ancient example of small clans finding strength through unity to avoid being overwhelmed by more powerful neighbours, such as the Macdonalds of the Isles.

Until this century, the chief of the Mackintoshes was also head of clan Chattan, but when the 28th Mackintosh chief, who was also the 29th Chattan chief, died in 1938 without a male heir, the two chiefships finally became separated. However, in 1947, the Lord Lyon ruled in favour of another branch of the Mackintoshes, those of Daviot, Inverness-shire, who were recognised as heads of clan Chattan. The present chief, Malcolm Kenneth Mackintosh, lives in Zimbabwe.

The clan Chattan is the second greatest Celtic community, after the Donalds, in the life and history of the Highlands. The clan name derives from that of its first chief, Gillichattan Mor, meaning the great servant of St.Catan, whose abbey was situated at Kilchattan on the island of Bute in the Firth of Clyde. The fourth chief had four sons, from whom, legend has it, four tribes descend. They were Gillichattan Patrick, the 5th Chief, Ewan Basn, ancestor of the clan Macpherson, Neil Crom, progenitor of the name Smith, and Farquhard Gilliriach, ancestor of the clan MacGillivray. The Mackintoshes themselves only appear on the scene through the marriage in 1291, of the 5th Chief's only child, Eva, to Angus Mackintosh, 6th chief of the clan Mackintosh, who then became, through his wife, the 7th chief of clan Chattan. Thereafter, membership of clan Chattan came to include seventeen tribes, plus the nine tribes of Mackintosh.

Trouble was fomented between the Mackintoshes and the Macphersons, with Macpherson of Cluny eventually matriculating the arms of the clan Chattan in his own right as its only true representative.

Members of the Mackintosh group include Farquharson, Macbean, MacGillivray, MacGlashan, MacHardie, MacQueen, Noble, MacTavish and Shaw. On the Macpherson side are Davidson, Gillespie, Keith and Smith. Others are Cattanach, Clark and Macphail.

The clan motto is "Touch not the cat without a glove" and the badge a rearing wild cat.

Sir Ivar Colquhoun of Luss is chief of the clan Colquhoun, named after land in Dunbartonshire granted in 1241. The bonny, bonny banks of Loch Lomond became part of the Colquhoun estates through a 14th-century marriage with a Celtic heiress. The 19th chief of the clan, Sir Iain, was one of the first to be granted a knighthood in the New World, when he became a Baron of Nova Scotia in 1625. This title was offered by James VI & I in return for financial help in establishing Scotland's first North American settlement.

The Colquhouns had to fight off other clans to keep their land. In 1439, one chief was killed by the Macleans of Duart on Inchmurrin, an island in Loch Lomond. His grandson, Iain, became Great Chamberlain of Scotland and Ambassador to England, and built the 15th-century Castle of Rossdhu, whose ruins can still be seen. The Colquhouns' greatest enemies were the raiding MacGregors, who massacred over 200 Colquhoun men in 1603 and carried off over 600 cattle and 280 horses, sheep and goats. A stone commemorating this bloody episode still stands on the site at Glenfruin, but a modern outcry has broken out over Ministry of Defence plans to remove it to make way for a temporary road to the nearby Trident nuclear submarine base.

After the Glenfruin massacre the MacGregors were outlawed by the King. But the Colquhouns never regained their military strength after this crippling blow, and their lands passed, on the marriage of the Colquhoun heiress, to the chief of the clan Grant in 1718. Over half a century later, James Grant was recognised as the 25th Colquhoun of Luss.

Much credit for preserving the scenic beauty of Loch Lomondside must go to the 20th-century Colquhoun chiefs, who have steadfastly refused to accept large sums of money for the commercial exploitation of their land.

Malcolm the Younger of Luss, heir to the chiefdom, married an American, Susan Timmerman from Harrisburg, Pennsylvania. His sister, Iona, is married to the 12th Duke of Argyll. Sir Ivar Colquhoun, the 28th Chief, lives on the clan's original lands, at Camstraddan, Luss, Dunbartonshire.

The clan motto is *Si Je Puis* — "If I can" and the badge is a hart's head. The war-cry, *Cnoc Ealachain*, is the name of a mountain.

TARTAN The Colquhoun tartan, with its deep blue background and white stripes, is very similar to the Leslie tartan.

Of all the clans who might have produced Kings of Scotland, the Cummings had the best chance, but they were pre-empted at the last moment. The first Cumming to arrive in Scotland came at exactly the right time, like Robert the Bruce's ancestor, with David I, who made this grandson of one of William the Conqueror's knights from Comines in Flanders the Chancellor of Scotland, and gave him Border lands in Roxburghshire.

The Cummings made all the right moves, such as marrying into the Celtic royal line and the ancient earldom of Buchan in the north. By 1286, they were the most powerful family in Scotland, ruling, as Lords of Badenoch, from their Castle in Lochindorb. They had a double claim to the Scottish throne, through the Celtic King Duncan and through the marriage of the Black Comyn (as the name was then spelt), to the Balliols who founded the Oxford college of that name and who produced a king of Scotland, John Balliol.

However, the man most likely to succeed to the Scottish throne, when it was left without a direct heir — John, the Red Comyn, son of the Black Comyn — was murdered in 1306 by Robert the Bruce before the altar of a Dumfries church, possibly because he was about to betray him to the King of England. Once Bruce became King, the Cummings were outlawed, their power destroyed and their estates parcelled out between Bruce's friends, the Douglases, the Keiths and the Hays, who had helped win the Battle of Bannockburn.

But one branch of the family, the Cummings of Altyre, Morayshire, descendants of Robert, the younger brother of the Black Comyn, managed to keep their lands intact for five centuries. These include the estates of Gordonstoun, after which the school attended by Prince Charles and his royal brothers is named. When Sir Alexander Cumming of Altyre was made a baronet in 1804 he took the name of Gordon Cumming from the estates of Gordonstoun. The present chief, the 22nd, is Sir William Gordon Cumming, who lives at Blairs House, Altyre, Forres in Morayshire.

The clan motto is "Courage" and the badge a lion rampant, holding a dagger in his paw.

TARTAN There is some confusion about the Cumming tartan. One version is the same as the MacAulay tartan, while another is like the MacIntyre. Three different versions are cited as tartans of the clan, under the different names of Cummin, Comyn, and Cumming. The version shown is a hunting tartan.

Though Davidson sounds a totally English name the clan is, in fact, a Gaelic tribe, one of the earliest to become associated with the confederation of the clan Chattan. The name comes from their leader, David Dubh of Invernahaven, who married a Mackintosh, daughter of the clan Chattan chief, in the mid-14th century, and, after the power vacuum created in the north-east by Bruce's defeat of the Cummings, sought protection in the Chattan numbers.

Unfortunately for the Davidsons, such an alignment brought them neither safety nor prosperity. They became involved in too many clan conflicts, getting caught in the middle of the struggle between the Mackintoshes and Macphersons for leadership of the clan Chattan. They are thought to be the clan Dhai who were almost annihilated in the famous 30-a-side clan battle fought on the North Inch at Perth in 1396 against the Macphersons. At the end only one member of the clan Dhai and eleven Macphersons were left alive. The hot-tempered clansmen were evidently battling over whether Davidson of Invernahaven as the oldest branch of the clan Chattan or Cluny Macpherson as its male heir should command the right wing of Chattan under its leader Mackintosh. After this disaster clan Dhai went into decline.

Tulloch Castle, a keep built in 1466 near Dingwall, Ross-shire, became the seat of the leading branch of the Davidsons through the marriage of Alexander Davidson of Davidson to its heiress, Miss Bayne of Tulloch, in the 18th century. There is a Davidson Association which has recorded its arms at the Lyon Court.

The clan motto is *Sapienter si sincere* — "Wisely if sincerely" — and the clan badge is a stag's head.

TARTAN There are two Davidson tartans, similar in design with dark green backgrounds. The earlier of the two tartans has an additional white stripe. This one is the later tartan.

Septs of the clan include Davey, Dawson, Day, Dean, Dow, Kay, MacDade, and Slora, while the Inverness-shire Mackays are said really to be MacDhais.

Douglas is another mighty name which resounds throughout the most purple pages of Scottish history, marrying into the royal family eleven times, and reaching the heights of political power, past and present. Most recently, Sir Alec Douglas-Home was Prime Minister of Great Britain in the 1960s, renouncing his hereditary title of Earl of Home to take his seat in the House of Commons, while his late nephew, Charles Douglas-Home, was editor of the London *Times* in the 1980s.

The Douglas-Homes, whose seat is the Hirsel, Coldstream, and the Dukes of Hamilton of Lennoxlove, near Haddington, now probably share the Douglas chiefship, since the arms and estates were merged with these two titles. The name, meaning "black stream", derives from the lands they were first granted in Lanarkshire in the 12th century, but their doughty part in the fight for Scottish independence, second only to that of the the fight for Scottish independence, second only to that of the patriots Wallace and Bruce, brought prominence to the "good Sir James" and generous gifts of estates from Bruce. The Black Douglas's exploits included three attacks on his own castle of Douglas when it was held by the English, and disguising his men as black oxen to capture Roxburgh. It was this greatest of Bruce's captains who was entrusted with taking Bruce's heart to the Holy Land, but was killed en route by the Moors in Spain.

The 4th Earl Douglas carried on the battle against England, both on the Borders and in France, where, as a general of Joan of Arc's Dauphin, he was made Duke of Touraine. By the 1450s this "over-mighty subject", who controlled the whole of south-west Scotland and could summon 30,000 men, was a threat to King James II, who murdered the 8th Earl of Douglas at Stirling in 1452 and then forfeited the estates and title of the 9th Earl in 1455, a turning-point in the fortunes of the Scottish crown.

Another Douglas, known as the Red Douglas, George Earl of Angus, took over when the Black Douglas was vanquished, this time siding with the crown against the Black Douglas clansmen and getting the estates back. Archibald, the 5th Earl of Angus, known as "Bell the Cat", was leader of the unruly barons who murdered James III's favourite. After the King himself was murdered in 1488, Archibald became guardian of the realm and Lord Chancellor. His grandson, the 6th Earl of Angus, married Margaret Tudor, James IV's widow, and the Douglases virtually ruled Scotland through keeping the young James V in their grasp until he escaped in 1528, ending their power.

The Douglases, though no longer at centre stage, still managed to gain more titles and honours through the centuries. The Angus Earldom had become the Dukedom of Douglas by 1703, but when, in 1761 the Duke died without an heir, the Angus titles went to the Duke of Hamilton. Similarly, in 1857 when the 4th Lord Douglas died, his niece, the Countess of Home, inherited the name and estates. In the 19th century, the Marquess of Queensberry, who gave his name to the boxing rules, was the father of Lord Alfred Douglas. Lord Alfred, known as "Bosie", was the notorious friend of the writer and poet, Oscar Wilde, and the cause of his downfall. These Douglases were descendants of the Drumlanrig branch of the family.

A humbler Douglas did much to change the landscape of Scotland by introducing into Britain the American tree named after him, the Douglas fir. David Douglas was a 27-year-old gardener, born in Scone, Perthshire, who explored the wild west of America, facing the hazards of Indians and bears, looking for plants and trees for the Horticultural Society of London. He brought back to Britain some 150 American plants and shrubs, but met an untimely death in Hawaii when he fell into a cattle-trap and was trampled to death by a wild bull.

The clan motto is *Jamais arrière* — "Never behind" — and its badge a salamander atop a burning hat.

TARTAN There are three Douglas tartans. The unusual black and grey check, shown here, is said to be linked to the Gaelic version of the name. The more traditional green and blue, with white stripes, is one of the other versions. Septs of the clan include Cavers, Forest, Glendinning, Inglis, Kirkpatrick, MacGuffie, Morton and Sandilands.

The Drummond motto, *Gang warily* — "Go Carefully" — and the spikes which form part of the chief's coat of arms are proud symbols of the clan's great military strategist who helped win Scotland's freedom on the field of Bannockburn. Sir Malcolm Drummond planted rows of spikes, concealed in pits, which impaled the English cavalry when they charged the smaller Scots army.

His rewards was honours and more land — the name of Drummond comes from Drymen, near Glasgow, with the chief, the Earl of Perth, still known today as *An Drumanach More*, "the great man of Drymen". The 17th Earl, who also has the title of Lord Drummond, still lives in the medieval mansion of Stobhall, near Perth, which came into the family when the 14th-century chief, John Drummond, married its heiress.

Two Queens of Scotland came from his family. His sister, Margaret, married Bruce's son, David II, but had no children, while his daughter, Annabella, became the wife of the second Stewart King, Robert III and was the mother of James I. The daughter of the first Lord Drummond almost became another Queen, since James IV was said to dote upon her, but she and her three sisters all died in mysterious circumstances, and are rumoured to have been poisoned. Instead James married Margaret Tudor, daughter of the English King Henry VII, which, a century later, led to the union of the Scottish and English crowns.

In 1605 the fourth Lord Drummond was made Earl of Perth; under James VII, the 4th Earl who, as Lord Chancellor, was chief administrator of Scotland, had the title of Duke of Perth bestowed upon him in exile. Always loyal to the Stewarts, the Drummond clan fared badly at Culloden. Lord Strathallan, a Drummond kinsman, was killed, and John, the 3rd Duke of Perth, was badly wounded and had to flee to France with his brother, who died at sea. Their estates were forfeited, but later restored in 1784.

With the death of the 6th Duke, the direct line ended, and the succession passed to a cousin, the eldest son of the Duke of Melfort, who became the 10th Earl of Perth. In 1800, the chieftaincy again reverted to the Duke of Melfort, a general in the French army, who died without issue; his brother, a Roman Catholic prelate, succeeded to the title. A nephew went before European courts to establish his right to the French titles and it required a British Act of Parliament in 1853 to restore his Scottish titles to him.

Even in this century the already extenuated line of succession was stretched again, back to the Strathallans, when the brother of the 11th Lord Strathallan became the 16th Earl of Perth. His European connections were internationally recognized when he was appointed was the first Secretary General of the League of Nations.

TARTAN There are three Drummond tartans. Some confusion exists about them since the Grant tartan is often called the Drummond. Certainly the Drummonds wore the Grant tartan during the Gathering of the Clans when George IV visited Edinburgh in 1822.

This is the Drummond of Perth tartan, similar to the one worn by Bonnie Prince Charlie as a cloak. Septs include Begg, Brewer, Cargill, Doig, Gruar, MacGrouther, MacRobbie and Robbie.

· DUNBAR ·

· ELLIOT ·

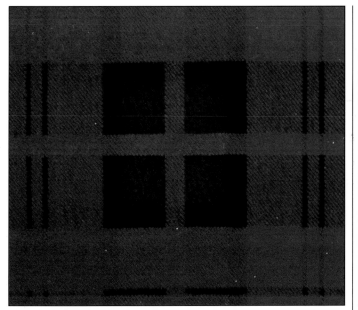

An American ex-jockey, Sir Jean Dunbar of Mochrum, is the chief of the clan Dunbar. Sir Jean was working as a cloth-cutter in New York's Lower East side when he inherited the title on the death of his father, Sir Adrian, the 12th Baronet. Sir Adrian himself was a colourful character, brought up in Canada, who joined the Australian army and married a Belgian. Now Sir Jean, who is known at his local race-track as "the Baron", lives in Fort Lauderdale, Florida. His son and heir, James Dunbar, is a captain in the American Air Force.

In 1983, the Lord Lyon, Scotland's King of Arms, held public court — for only the third time this century — to adjudicate on the claim by 90-year-old Colonel William Dunbar of Herne Bay, Kent. As half-brother of the 11th Baronet, Sir Richard Dunbar, who had died only two days after succeeding to the title, Colonel William claimed to be the rightful heir. His father had caused the complications by marrying twice, but the Lord Lyon ruled that the Colonel could not succeed to the title.

Ironically, because of a similar 15th-century marriage tangle the Dunbars failed to inherit the Earldom of Moray after the murder in 1429 of the fourth Earl. Instead the Earldom passed down through his daughters, while the descendant of his son by a second marriage became the 1st Baronet of Mochrum in 1694. Mr. Hugh Peskett, research director of *Burke's Peerage*, claimed during the Lyon court hearings that if Colonel Dunbar's case suceeded, then the Dunbars might also be able to claim the Earldom of Moray.

As it is, the Dunbars can claim an unbroken male descent for more than 1,000 years and 33 generations, back to Duncan, the lay Abbot of Dunkeld, killed in battle in 965 and probably descended from the ancient Kings of Ulster. King Malcolm III gave the lands of Dunbar to Gospatric, nephew of King Duncan I, making him Earl of Dunbar in 1072. Patrick, the 9th Earl, married Agnes, daughter of the 1st Earl of Moray, the redoubtable "Black Agnes" of history who stalwartly defended Dunbar Castle against an English siege in 1337. A ballad describes her as a "brawling, boisterous Scottish wench", but after succeeding as Countess of Moray, she died childless, and the Dunbar title passed to the Morays.

The clan motto is "Honour is the prize of honesty" and the badge is a white horse's head.

TARTAN This old tartan has a red background with green and black checks.

There are several ways of spelling this name, which may be derived from the village of Eliot, Forfar (the form used by the 20th-century poet, T.S. Eliot). The present clan chief's name has an additional *t*. He is Sir Arthur Eliott of Stobs, who lives at Redheugh, Newcastleton, in the Borders, where a near neighbour, Baroness Elliot of Harwood, a life peer in her own right has the most generally used version of the name. Her late husband, Walter Elliot, one of Scotland's outstanding 20th-century politicians, helped to save the blazing medieval Westminster Hall when the House of Commons was bombed in 1941.

The Elliots were one of the Border clans in the turbulent 15th century, when the chief of that time, whose name was spelt differently yet again, Robert Elwood, was keeper of Hermitage Castle in Roxburghshire, the great stronghold of the Douglases. Now restored, it had a long, cruel history; Mary, Queen of Scots nearly died here of a fever, after riding from Jedburgh and back, some forty miles, all in one day.

The Eliot of Stobs branch was recognized as the major branch. In 1700 Gilbert Eliot was created 1st Baronet of Minto. His sister Jane achieved everlasting fame by composing the song *The Flowers of the Forest*, the lament for the men lost at Flodden. The next Gilbert was made an Earl and became Governor-General of India in 1807, an appointment emulated by the 4th Earl Minto, who was Viceroy of India from 1905 to 1910, after having served as Governor-General of Canada.

In the 18th century, George Elliot, son of the 3rd Baronet, also served the British cause by raising a regiment of light horse, initially named for him, but later to become the King's Royal Regiment of Light Dragoons. He became a General and, as Governor of Gibraltar, fought off over 100, 000 French and Spanish troops and four dozen ships to keep the Rock British. For this feat he was knighted Lord Heathfield, Baron of Gibraltar.

The clan motto is *Fortitor et recte* — "With strength and right" — and the badge is an armoured hand holding a broadsword.

TARTAN As a Border clan the Elliots have no Highland associations and their tartan, an attractive bright blue background with maroon checks, is of more recent origin.

Chief of the Erskine family is the Earl of Mar & Kellie (13th Earl of Mar & 15th Earl of Kellie), who lives at Claremont House, Alloa, Clackmannanshire. The name comes from estates in Renfrewshire. The Erskines married into the Celtic Earldom of the land of Mar, which dates from the 13th century, but were stripped of the title in 1457.

That is why today there are, rather confusingly, two Scottish Earldoms of Mar. The newer of the two was conferred in 1565 by Mary, Queen of Scots, who rewarded John Erskine for his custodianship of her father, herself, and her own infant child before they reached their majority, while also restoring the ancient Earldom of Mar to him. The two titles were split yet again after the 28th and 9th Earl of Mar died without issue in 1866.

The 6th Earl of Mar raised the standard in 1715 for the 1st Jacobite rising and, fleeing to France, was made titular Duke of Mar by James VII. The Earls of Buchan and of Rosslyn are also descended from the Erskine family. Three holders of the Erskine baronetcy of Cambo have held the office of Lord Lyon, Scotland's King of Arms.

The clan motto is *Je pense plus* — "I think more". The badge shows a hand holding a dagger.

TARTAN The Erskine tartan has green checks on a red background and is one of the first Lowland tartans to be recorded. A green Erskine tartan has also been invented this century.

The chief of the clan Farquharson, Alwyne Farquharson of Invercauld, is a next-door neighbour of Queen Elizabeth II, for he lives at Braemar on royal Deeside. In fact, the Farquharsons originally owned Balmoral — now a summer residence of the British Royal Family — until it passed to the Gordons, from whom Prince Albert bought it in 1852 to make it into Queen Victoria's beloved Scottish home.

The Farquharsons have been on friendly terms with royalty for many centuries. Mary, Queen of Scots, presented a clarsach — a little harp — to Beatrix Farquharson, whose husband, Finlay, was killed carrying the Royal Standard at the battle of Pinkie in 1547. This clarsach, which Beatrix evidently played beautifully, was later owned by the Robertsons of Lude, who also had the Lamont harp, possibly a century older. Both harps are now in Edinburgh's Royal Museum of Scotland, sole survivors of the Celtic musical instrument which the Scots and Irish once shared.

A 17th-century document shows that the Farquharsons of Invercauld descended from the tribe of Shaw, part of the clan Chattan confederation, and from the MacDuffs, Thanes of Fife. Farquhar, son of Shaw of Rothiemurchus, moved to Aberdeenshire and his son married the heiress of Invercauld. Their son, Finlay Mor, killed as the royal standard-bearer, was the first of the house of Farquharson of Invercauld. Ever afterwards the Farquharsons have been called *Clann Fhionnlaigh* — descendants of Finlay.

In the first Jacobite rising of 1715, John Farquharson joined the clan Chattan with 140 men and 4 officers, and was taken prisoner. In the '45 the Farquharsons with their 300 men were in the front line at Culloden. But later descendants joined the Hanoverian army.

The line has twice passed through the female succession, the present chief inheriting the title from his aunt, Mrs. Myrtle Farquharson.

The clan motto is *Fide et fortitudine* — "By fidelity and fortitude". The badge shows the upper half of a lion rampant, with a sword in his paw.

TARTAN This is one of the two forms of the Farquharson tartan. Both are said to be based on the Black Watch regimental tartan, the major difference being the positioning of the red and yellow stripes. There are many septs of this clan, including Barrie, Christie, Coates, Findlay, Gracie, Hardy, Lyon, Macartney, Macerchar, Mackinlay, Paterson and Reoch.

The chief of the clan is Sir Charles Fergusson (the other way of spelling the name) of Kilkerran, who lives at Maybole, Ayrshire. His uncle, Sir Bernard Fergusson, was the leader of the Chindits in Burma during World War II, and later became Governor-General of New Zealand.

Kilkerran, the name of the chief's seat, is the ancient name for the modern Campbeltown in Kintyre, where the Fergusons are said to have first settled. St. Ciaran, one of the Twelve Apostles of Ireland, landed there in the 6th century, and the Fergussons of Kilkerran may be the descendants of Fergus, who was the keeper of St. Ciaran's cross. Sir John Fergusson of Kilkerran was created a Baronet in 1703.

Another branch, the Fergusons of Craigdarroch, Dumfriesshire, claim 12th-century descent from Fergus, Prince of Galloway, and their family lands can be dated back to the 15th century. This was the family into which Annie Laurie of Maxwelton, the bonnie Annie Laurie of the song, married.

Argyllshire, too, was another ancient seat of the Clann Fhearghuis of Strachur, Loch Fyneside. The last known representative of this branch, Seumas, may be somewhere in the United States, as his only known address is the Explorers Club, New York. The Fergusons of Balquidder, Perthshire, can trace their ancestry back for six centuries, the oldest families being those of Ardandamh, Strathyre, Loch Lubnaig and Immervoulin. They have a tartan of their own. Finally, there are the Fergusons of Aberdeenshire, landowners since the 14th century, whose most prominent families are those of Baddifurrow, Kinmundy and Pitfour.

During the American War of Independence, a member of the clan, Dr. Adam Ferguson, Professor of Mathematics and Natural Philosophy at Edinburgh University, was sent across the Atlantic to try and make terms with the rebel colonists in 1778. Later, he became a close friend of the novelist, Sir Walter Scott.

Robert Burns so admired the verse of his fellow Scottish poet, Robert Fergusson, an Aberdeenshire bank clerk's son who died in an insane asylum aged only 23, that, poor as he himself was, he sought out Fergusson's unmarked grave and had a monument erected over it. Burns' tribute can still be seen today in the Canongate Kirk graveyard, in Edinburgh's Royal Mile.

The clan's motto is *Dulcius ex aspersis* — "Sweeter after difficulties". The badge is a bee atop a thistle.

TARTAN There are two distinct Ferguson tartans, the Ferguson of Balquhidder, and this one, the Ferguson of Athol, which closely resembles the MacLaren tartan, possibly because both these clans followed the Murrays of Atholl.

The clan's present chief, the 23rd Lord Forbes, the premier Baron of Scotland, lives at Balforbes, Alford, Aberdeenshire, the Donside area where the clan originated as early as the 13th century. Two hundred years after Sir Alexander Forbes married into the royal line of King Robert III and was made Lord Forbes in 1445, his descendant, the 10th Lord, was evidently living in very straitened circumstances, due to being constantly menaced by their neighbours, the Gordons.

Other branches of the Forbes family prospered and built some of the finest Scottish tower houses. The gem is the fairy-tale castle of Craigievar, all turrets and spires, built in 1626 by "Danzig" William Forbes, a timber merchant, and bought by benefactors from the Forbes-Sempill family for the National Trust for Scotland in 1963. The massive ruined castle of Tolquhoun, near Tarves, was built in the 1580s by a very old branch of the Forbes family who acquired their lands in 1420. The five towers of Fyvie Castle enshrine five centuries of Scottish history, each built by the five families who have owned this castle, which dates from the 13th century. It was bought from the Forbes-Leith family by the National Trust for Scotland, who consider it to be the grandest example of Scottish baronial architecture.

The Forbes played leading roles on both sides during the Jacobite risings. Lord Forbes of Culloden, Lord President of the Court of Session, Scotland's leading judge, is said to have saved the Hanoverian throne through his powerful influence in swaying some Highland chiefs not to follow Bonnie Prince Charlie. Lord Pitsligo, another Forbes, on the other hand was out in both the 1715 and 1745 and, as a hunted rebel, had, literally, a hair-raising escape. An elderly Miss Gordon hid the septuagenarian Lord behind her bed, and while government soldiers felt her chin to make sure she was not a man, she coughed loudly — to drown Pitsligo's heavy breathing.

The clan motto is "Grace me Guide", and the badge is a stag's head.

TARTAN There are three versions of the Forbes tartan. Miss Forbes of Pitsligo is said to have created this one by changing the yellow line of the regimental Gordon tartan to white in 1822, producing a tartan which is almost identical to the Lamont design. While the Forbes dress tartan could be taken for the hunting tartan of Cluny Macpherson, the third tartan is similar to that of the Black Watch.

Septs of the Forbes clan include Bannerman, Berry, Fordyce, Lumsden, MacQuat, MacOwat, Mekie, Middleton, Walter, Watson, Watt, and Wattie.

Today's chief of the clan Fraser is Lady Saltoun — 20th holder of the title which was created in 1445 — who lives at Cairnbulg Castle, Aberdeenshire. She married Captain Alexander Ramsay, of Mar, whose mother was a grand-daughter of Queen Victoria, and her daughter and heir to the chiefship, the Hon. Mrs. Katherine Nicolson, is a third cousin of the Queen.

Chief of the major branch of the Frasers, Simon, 15th Lord Lovat, who was a World War II commando, winning many foreign military honours, lives at Balblair House, Beauly, Inverness-shire, and owns around 190,000 acres of the area where the clan settled. Chief of this clan is always known as *MacShimi* (son of Simon) after its founder, a younger son of Sir Alexander Fraser, progenitor of the Saltoun line.

Originally the Frasers came from France — La Frézelière in Anjou is the origin of the name — and settled first in East Lothian, becoming a Highland clan after the Scottish fight for independence from England when Edward I invaded Scotland in 1296. Frasers played a heroic part in the battles. Sir Simon Fraser, a supporter of William Wallace, was captured fighting for Robert the Bruce and was hung, drawn and quartered.

Sir Alexander Fraser, founder of the Saltoun line, married Robert the Bruce's sister, Mary and became Lord Chamberlain of Scotland. In 1375 their grandson acquired the castle of Cairnbulg and the lands of Philorth in Buchan through marriage with Joanna, daughter of the Earl of Ross. In the 16th century Sir Alexander, 8th Earl of Philorth, founded Fraserburgh, now one of the major North Sea oil and fishing ports, and almost succeeded in setting up a university there, but Aberdeen was not prepared to have such a close academic rival. His son, also called Alexander, married the heiress of Saltoun, and Saltoun has been the title of the chiefs of the clan Fraser ever since.

Their chiefship was disputed by the head of another branch, who had been created Lord Fraser by Charles I in 1633 and had built Castle Fraser (now in the care of the National Trust for Scotland) in Grampian, but the 4th Lord Fraser was a Jacobite and died a fugitive after 1715.

Lord Lovat, known as "the old fox", hesitated about supporting Bonnie Prince Charlie in '45, but sent his son to command the clan at Culloden. The "Old Fox", aged 80, was later imprisoned and executed, while his son was eventually pardoned. In 1757 he raised the 1800 men of the Fraser Highlanders who fought in America and, as General Simon Fraser, was in command when they captured Quebec. A later namesake explored the Fraser river in Canada.

The clan motto is *Je suis prest* — "I am ready". The badge is a buck's head.

Septs of this clan are numerous and include Abernethy, Bisset, Cowie, Frisell, Gruar, Macillrick, MacSimon, Mactavish, Simpson, Sym and Tweedie.

TARTAN The most popular of the Fraser tartans has a red background with green checks and a white stripe, though it may not be as genuine as the other two. These are the clan Fraser and the very similar Fraser of Lovat, only distinguishable by the way the green and white lines are centred. This modern hunting Fraser tartan has a brown background in place of the red.

⋄ G O R D O N ⋄

Chief of this north-eastern clan is the Marquis of Huntly, premier Marquess of Scotland, who lives at Aboyne Castle, Aberdeenshire. His heir is the Earl of Aboyne. This territorial name was taken north from lands in the south of Scotland by Anglo-Normans who had settled there in the 12th century, but so powerful did they become in the Highlands that the chief is still known as "Cock o'the North".

The senior male line died out but an heiress married into another powerful line, that of the Setons, and their son was created Earl of Huntly in 1445, gaining the former Cumming lands of Badenoch. This was the time when the Scottish crown was weak and the Gordons virtually ruled the Northeast as the Campbells did the West. After Flodden, the Gordons' most spectacular coup was to seize the Earldom of Sutherland in 1514.

When Mary, Queen of Scots, offered the Earldom of Moray, which the Gordons coveted, to her half-brother, they rebelled and were defeated by Mary's troops at Corrichie in 1562. The Earl of Huntly, gross, corpulent and short of breath, died on the field of a stroke, and his son, John, was beheaded in Aberdeen. But James VI & I (of Scotland and England) restored power to the Gordons, making the Earl a Marquess. The Gordons later seized the Mackay lands of Strathnaver and attacked the Sinclair Earldom of Caithness.

The 2nd Marquess was beheaded by the Covenanters. The 4th Marquess was created Duke of Gordon in 1684 by Charles II, a title which died with the 5th Duke in 1836, while the Marquisate passed to the Earl of Aboyne. Other members of this family were longer-lived. The nonagenarian 9th Marquess of Huntly survived to dance both with Marie Antoinette, who particularly admired his Highland Fling, and with Queen Victoria.

Another branch of the clan, the Gordons of Haddo, also acquired great distinction and were also long-lived. Patrick, the 3rd of Haddo, received charters to his lands from three Kings, James III, IV and V. John, the 5th of Haddo, was made a Baronet by Charles I for his part in the Battle of Turriff in 1642. The following year, he was captured and imprisoned in Edinburgh's St. Giles Cathedral, where a recess is still known as Haddo's Hole. He was the first royalist to be judicially sentenced to execution and died in 1644. The family fortunes were later restored and the 3rd Lord Haddo was made Lord High Chancellor and created Earl of Aberdeen in 1682.

The Earls of Aberdeen became prominent political leaders. The 4th Earl was Prime Minister of Great Britain from 1852 to 1855, at the time of the Crimean War, while the 7th Earl, who died in 1934, was Governor-General of Canada and was made a Marquess. 18th-century Haddo House, an early Adam masterpiece, is now the setting for musical concerts and was conveyed to the National Trust for Scotland by the 4th Marquess.

Two regiments were raised from this clan. The old 81st was raised in 1777, and disbanded in 1783. The 4th Duke of Gordon, and his celebrated Duchess Jane, raised the 92nd or Gordon Highlanders in 1794.

The clan motto is *Bydand* — "Remaining" — and the badge a buck's head above a coronet.

TARTAN When the Gordon Highlanders were raised, a yellow line was added to the Black Watch tartan to make a new regimental tartan. This was then adopted by the clan Gordon. When the Gordon tartan became the regimental tartan of the Gordon Highlanders, this Huntly tartan became the Gordon dress tartan.

The 7th Duke of Montrose, Rhodesian Minister of Defence from 1965 to 1968, who lives in Salisbury, Zimbabwe, is chief of this clan. His heir, the Marquess of Graham, who married a Canadian, stays in Scotland near the former family seat of Buchanan Castle, at Drymen, near Glasgow. The 6th Duke of Montrose, who married the daughter of the 12th Duke of Hamilton, had lived at Brodick Castle on the island of Arran, an ancient stronghold of the Hamiltons. After his death, Brodick Castle, parts of which date back to the 13th century, was accepted in lieu of death duties in 1958, and is now in the care of the National Trust for Scotland.

Traditionally, the Grahams claim descent from a Caledonian chief who repelled the Romans, but the first authenticated record is of William de Grahame, who witnessed David I's foundation of Holyrood Abbey in 1158 and may have travelled to Scotland with him. After being granted lands, first in Abercorn and Dalkeith, near Edinburgh, the Grahams later married into a royal Celtic family with lands at Strathearn in Perthshire.

The tradition of military bravery, which has earned them the soubriquet of the "gallant Grahams", began as early as the 13th century, when Sir Patrick Graham died carrying the royal banner in the Wars of Independence. His nephew, Sir John, was William Wallace's right-hand man, and also fell in battle at Falkirk.

William, the 3rd Lord Graham, who was made Earl of Montrose in 1505, died at Flodden. Perhaps the greatest soldier of them all was the 5th Earl, who became Marquis of Montrose in 1644. At first he had supported the Covenanters who rebelled against the high-church policies of Charles I. However, he began to suspect that the Marquis of Argyll was trying to supplant the crown, so he supported the king, fighting a brilliant royalist campaign in the Highlands. With the help of the Macdonalds, he gained the reputation of Europe's leading general.

Montrose, the poet-soldier who wrote the famous verses "He either fears his fate too much, or his deserts are small, that dares not put it to the touch, to gain or lose it all", was captured in 1650. As he was led up Edinburgh's Royal Mile to the scaffold, his enemy, the Marquis of Argyll, who happened to be celebrating his son's wedding to the Earl of Moray's daughter, jeered at him from the balcony of Moray House. Edinburgh Town council still has the accounts for the cost of new gallows (£12. 8s. 4d.) and for sharpening the axe (12s.) to quarter the body. Yet only 10 years later Argyll was to meet the same fate himself on the Edinburgh scaffold. When Charles II was restored to the throne, the remains of Montrose, whose poem, written on the eve of his execution, ended with the hope that he would be raised with the just, were given a magnificent state burial.

Yet another member of the clan, Graham of Claverhouse, Viscount Dundee — "Bonnie Dundee" to his admirers, "Bloody Claverhouse" to his enemies — died fighting for the Stewart Kings at the pass of Killiecrankie in 1689.

James Graham, later the 3rd Duke of Montrose, fought a very different kind of battle on behalf of the Highlanders. He won back their right to wear the tartan and play the bagpipes by piloting a bill through Parliament in 1782 which repealed the 1747 prohibition on Highland dress.

The septs of Graham of Montrose are Bonar, Bonnar and Grahame. Those of Graham of Menteith, another branch of the clan, include Allardyce, Blair, Bontine, Haldane, MacGibbon, Monteath, and Pye.

The clan motto is *Ne oublie* — "Do not forget" — and the badge is a winged falcon attacking a stork.

TARTAN There are three Graham tartans. Both the Graham of Montrose, shown here, and the Graham of Menteith resemble the MacCallum tartans but it is not clear who borrowed from whom. The older Graham tartan, a simple design of greens and blacks, was never generally used.

Sir Patrick Grant of Grant, 5th Lord Strathspey, 32nd chief of the clan, lives at Elms Cottage, Elms Ride, West Wittering, Sussex. The clan's territories are on Speyside, amid the magnificent scenery of the Cairngorm Mountains and the straths of Glenurquhart and Glenmoriston beside Loch Ness. The clan gathering place is at Ballintome, near Glenmoriston, while its war-cry — "Stand fast, Craigellachie" — comes from a rock near Aviemore. A Strathspey moor, *Griantach*, may be the origin of the clan's name.

One theory is that the Grants are descended from the 12th-century clan More ("great" in Gaelic) McGregor. This would make it one of the principal branches of the *Siol Alpine*, the stock of the Pictish King, Kenneth McAlpine, of which clan Gregor is the chief. The Grants were sheriffs of Inverness from the 13th century, holding sway in northeast Scotland, with Sir Ian Grant, sheriff in 1434, the first chief from whom authenticated descent can be traced.

His grandson, also John, known as "the gentle" Grant, was with Mary, Queen of Scots, when her musician, Rizzio, was murdered before her eyes. Two generations later, his grandson was offered the peerage of Strathspey by Mary's son, King James VI, but refused it saying: "Wha'll be the Laird o'Grant?" (Who will be the Lord of Grant?) However, in 1663, with the Grants' powers increasing, as those of the Gordons waned in the North, James, the 7th of Freuchie, did accept the title of Strathspey, but died before it could be conferred upon him.

Freuchie was re-named Castle Grant, and this old 16th-century mansion can still be seen near Granton-on-Spey, the Highland town the Grants established in 1766 in the midst of their estates as an agricultural and industrial centre.

There are five branch clans, clan Allan (Grant of Auchernack) clan *Phadraig* (Grant of Tullochgorum), clan Donnachie (Grant of Gartenbeg) and clan Chiaran (Grant of Dellachapple), with three Grant baronetcies, of Dalvey, Monymust and Ballindalloch.

The clan motto is "Stand fast" and the badge the rock of Craigellachie in flames. General Ulysses Grant, President of the United States from 1868 to 1876, was said to have bet that he could keep an emotionless poker face but lost when the clan rallying cry of "Stand fast, Graigellachie" was shouted.

TARTAN This is the more commonly worn of the two Grant tartans; it is sometimes wrongly thought of as the Drummond tartan. The Black Watch tartan is worn as a hunting tartan, while the Grant of Monymusk is made from Huntly tartans.

The history of the clan Gunn vividly illustrates the saddest episode in Scotland's past, the Highland Clearances (see page 70) which dispersed the Gunns, along with many other Highlanders, throughout the world. They originally lived principally in the Sutherland glens of Kildonan. Some Gunns founded a new Kildonan in Canada, others went to New Zealand. Those who stayed behind had to move to the coastal villages and learn new skills as fishermen. The Gunns had come from Caithness. They may have been a Pictish tribe, though they claim descent from the Norse King of Man, Olave the Black. They were a warlike bunch, constantly crossing swords with their neighbours, the Keiths; one theory is that their name comes from the Norse *Gunnr*, meaning war.

Their belligerence eventually led to their having to move to Sutherland during the 15th and 16th centuries. That was after the Gunn chief, the colourful George Gunn, coroner (royal lawyer) of Caithness, who lived in great Celtic style in his Castle of Clyth, near Wick, had been outwitted by the Keiths. To settle their feud — which may have started when a beautiful Gunn heiress called Helen was abducted by a rejected Keith suitor and later leapt to her death from his tower — the Gunn and Keith chiefs agreed in 1464 to meet with 12 horsemen a side. But the Keiths galloped up with 24 men, two on each horse, and cut the Gunns to pieces, including the chief, whom they stripped of his arms and silver brooch (pin) of office.

After that George's eldest son, James, moved to Strathullie in Sutherland and founded the branch named after him — MacSeamus or MacKeamish. His other sons also established new families, with Henry becoming the progenitor of the Hendersons of Caithness, while the Williamsons and Wilsons of Caithness are traditionally said to be named after William Gunn. By the end of the 16th century the Gunns were listed among the "broken clans" of the North, described as very courageous, but more desperate than violent. In the 20th century, the novelist Neil Gunn, son of an east coast fisherman, has written graphically about Scottish herring fishing, in a book called *The Silver Darlings*.

The clan motto is *Aut pax aut bellum* — "Either peace or war". The badge is a right hand holding a sword.

TARTAN The Gunn tartan has a light green ground with black and blue bands and red stripes.

The 15th Duke of Hamilton. Scotland's premier peer and hereditary keeper of the Royal Palace of Holyrood in Edinburgh, is chief of the Hamiltons, a family which has always been closely connected with the crown. Twice, in fact, the Hamiltons have stood next in line to the throne. After James, the 1st Lord Hamilton, married Princess Mary, daughter of James II in 1474, their descendants for a century thereafter stood to inherit the crown if the Kings, often minors, should die.

In the 19th century, the 10th Duke, who claimed to be the legitimate heir of the Stewart dynasty which had ended in 1807, lived like a prince in the great Hamilton Palace in Lanarkshire. With the wealth brought by the neighbouring coal mines, he vied with the Prince Regent, later George IV, in collecting French works of art for the remodelled palace. The Duke commissioned a painting of Napoleon whom he greatly admired (now in Washington's National Gallery). He subsequently became a close friend of Napoleon's sister, Princess Pauline Borghese, who left him her travelling chest, filled with silver cutlery, toilet articles and needlework when she died. In preparation for his own death, this very Duke of Dukes commissioned a neo-classical mausoleum beside the palace, which is said to have been the most costly and magnificent temple ever built for the dead in Europe, and left instructions that his body was to be embalmed. Ironically, the coal mines which had enabled him to live like a king also caused the downfall of the palace, which subsided through under-mining and had to be demolished in the 1920s, though the mausoleum was bought by the town of Hamilton. In continuing the ties with the Bonaparte family, the 11th Duke married a cousin of Napoleon.

Although the Hamilton lands were originally in Lanarkshire (where the modern town of Hamilton is today) the name is said to come from Hamildoun in Northumberland. Their barony of Cadzow, where a ruined castle overlooking the Clyde still remains today and from which a famous herd of Scottish wild cattle took its name, was granted by Robert the Bruce. Thereafter the Hamiltons stayed loyal to the crown and prospered.

Always a Lowland family, from 1503 they lived at Brodick Castle on the island from which their title of Earl of Arran came.

The 2nd Earl of Arran was Regent of Scotland, Guardian of the young Mary, Queen of Scots, and putative heir to the throne if she had no children. However, he was accused of switching sides for personal gain whenever it suited him between the English and the French, who were both vying for control of the Scottish crown. Though he was presented with the French Dukedom of Chatelherault, he was deposed in favour of Mary of Guise, Mary Queen of Scots' mother, while Frenchmen were put in charge of Scottish finances and the Great Seal of Scotland. Secretly, too, the 15-year-old Queen signed three documents assigning her country to the King of France if she should die childless, even before her marriage to the Dauphin, the heir to the French throne. This danger of France taking over Scotland was one of the causes of the 16th-century Protestant revolution in Scotland, led by John Knox.

As ardent royalists, later Hamiltons were to lose their lives, including the 1st Duke of Hamilton, executed in 1649, while only two years later his brother, the 2nd Duke, died fighting for Charles II at Worcester. His niece, Anne, who became the 3rd Duchess of Hamilton, married the Earl of Selkirk, a title which later passed to her second son. The Irish Dukedom of Abercorn was a title which was conferred on another branch of the Hamilton family, while the Hamiltons of Innerwick became the Earls of Haddington.

The 14th Duke, father of the present Duke of Hamilton, achieved the rare distinction in 1933 of being the first pilot to fly over Everest. The present Duke is also a pilot, having been in the R.A.F. and a test pilot for Scottish Aviation.

The clan motto is "Through" and the badge is an oak tree, penetrated by a frame saw, standing above a ducal coronet.

TARTAN The Hamilton tartan, a family one only, has a red background with blue checks and white stripes. There is also a hunting tartan with a green background.

The chief of the clan Hay, the 24th Earl of Erroll, as the hereditary Lord High Constable of Scotland, a title bestowed upon the family of Hay by Robert the Bruce, takes precedence over all other holders of hereditary titles in Scotland except those of royal blood. The Earl, a computer consultant who lives in Hampshire, England, also has jurisdiction over all matters of affray within a four-mile radius of the Queen when she is in Scotland.

The Hays were Normans who rose rapidly to power in Scotland by being trusted by the crown and by marrying into the old Pictish and Celtic aristocracy. They were also well rewarded by Robert the Bruce with lands in Slains, Aberdeenshire, to add to their 12th-century Perthshire estates. The 1st Lord Erroll was Butler (royal cup-bearer) of Scotland, while the 5th Earl was made the Lord High Constable, a remarkable ascendancy in just over 150 years, to become one of the most powerful Scottish families.

Despite their early success, the Hays' stronghold of Slains Castle, near Ellon, Aberdeenshire, was demolished personally by James VI after Erroll, in a Catholic conspiracy allied with Huntly, defeated the Earl of Argyll in 1594 and threatened Aberdeen with the sword. The 13th Earl opposed the Union of Scotland and England in 1707, and was an early supporter of the Jacobites. His sister, Mary, the 14th Countess, and an even more dedicated Jacobite, used the rebuilt castle of Slains as a centre for Jacobite espionage and raised the clan to battle in 1745. She was succeeded in 1758 by her great-nephew, Lord Boyd, whose loyalty to the Stewart cause had caused the clan to be stripped of three titles. Yet at the Great Gathering of the Clans when George IV visited Edinburgh in 1822, William, the 18th Earl of Erroll, was so magnificently arrayed as Lord High Constable that the family coffers were almost emptied.

The clan Hay's centre is at Delgatie Castle, Turriff, Aberdeenshire, seat of a cadet branch. Other cadet branches include the Earls of Kinnoull and the Marquesses of Tweeddale. James Hay, Earl of Carlisle, owned the Carlisle Islands, annexed to the crown in the 17th century, and now known as Barbados.

The clan motto is *Serva jugem* — "Keep the yoke". The badge shows a falcon flying. The coat of arms shows farm implements which, legend has it, were the weapons by which the Hays repelled a Danish invasion at Luncarty.

TARTAN The Hays have two tartans. This one is called Hay and Leith because it was evidently also used by the Leith family. The other tartan, resembling the Drummond, is more generally worn. Septs include Constable, Gifford and Mackester.

Though originally a Highland clan, holding lands in Morayshire from the 12th century, the 30th Innes chief, the 10th Duke of Roxburgh, lives in magnificent Floors castle at Kelso, in the Scottish Borders. The Innes Clan Trust has in its possession Edder-Innes in the heart of the old clan country.

A Flemish knight called Berowald was the first to take the name Innes from the Morayshire estate which King Malcolm IV gave him in 1160. This included the rich farming lands between the rivers Spey and Lossie, which the Innes, seen as worthy lairds, kept and expanded for the next 600 years. It was Bishop Innes, son of the 8th Baronet, who rebuilt Elgin Cathedral, the most northerly on the mainland, in the 15th century after it had been destroyed by the "Wolf of Badenoch", son of King Robert II. The 19th Baronet founded Garmouth on the Spey in 1587.

The Innes clan also produced some outstanding scholars, like the 18th-century Principal of the Scots College in Paris, Father Lewis, who saved many Scottish medieval records. So too did Cosmo Innes, a professor at Edinburgh University in the 19th century. Others became politicians, like the 15th chief who sat in the Reformation Parliament of 1560, while the 20th chief, the member of parliament for Moray, was both a prominent Covenanter and a faithful supporter of Charles II, who gave him Speymouth in 1650. Two earlier chiefs met untimely ends: the 16th, who killed a clansman at Edinburgh's Cross, was beheaded by the Regent Morton, and the 18th was murdered.

Sir Robert, the 20th chief, was one of the first Baronets of Nova Scotia, and it was the marriage of the 3rd Baronet, Sir James, to Lady Margaret Ker which led to his great-grandson, Sir James, inheriting the Roxburghe Dukedom through the maternal line in 1805. Proud of his Innes ancestry, this 5th Duke privately printed the details of his family in 1820 "to show those proud Kers that he was of as good blood on his father's side as on his great-grandmother's".

Guy Innes-Ker, the 10th Duke and present chief, has two sons and a daughter. Cadet branches in the North include Sir Berowald Innes, 16th Baronet of Balvenie, Banffshire, and Sir Charles Innes, 11th Baronet of Coxton, Morayshire.

The clan motto is *Be traist* — "Be faithful". The badge is a boar's head.

TARTAN There are two Innes tartans, one hunting and the dress tartan shown here. They are shared with the MacInnes. Septs include Inch, MacRob, and Reidfurd.

The Johnstones are principally a Border clan though there is a separate northern clan of different origins. First mention of the surname comes in the 13th century, when it was taken from the lands of Johnston in Annandale by Sir Gilbert de Johnstoun. The title of Earl of Annandale, conferred upon the Johnstones in 1661, became dormant but has recently been revived and granted to Hope-Johnstone, chief of the Border clan, whose seat is at Raehills, Lockerbie, Dumfriesshire.

American-based Sir Thomas Johnston, the 13th Baronet of Caskieben, Aberdeenshire, is descended from Stephen the Clerk, who married Margaret, the heiress of Sir Andrew Garioch, in the 14th century and succeeded to the lands of Johnston in the North. In 1626, his descendant, George Johnston, became a Baronet of Nova Scotia. Sir Thomas, the present head, a former member of the Alabama State Senate, lives in Mobile.

The Johnstones are remembered as a brawling, boisterous Border clan, one of the most aggressive in the western area of those disputed, cattle-raiding territories, whose main rivals were the Douglas and Maxwell clans. The Devil's Beef Tub, a dramatic hollow in the upper Annandale hills near Moffat, ideal for secreting rustled cattle, became known as "the beef-stand of the Johnstones". Sir Walter Scott described them as "a race of uncommon hardihood".

Later generations stayed loyal to the crown; Sir James Johnstone was made Lord Johnstone by Charles I in 1633, and Earl of Hartfell 10 years later. His son was made the Earl of Annandale, and his grandson Marquess of Annandale in 1701. After the direct male line died out in 1792 the title passed through marriage to the 1st Earl of Hopetoun, from whom the Hope-Johnstones, whose claim to the Annandale title has now been proved, are descended.

The legal skills of Archibald Johnston of Warriston, a member of the Annandale family, produced the National Covenant. This was a move to defend the true religion of Scotland after Charles I made himself head of the Church in 1635 and introduced a "papist" liturgy which provoked the celebrated riot in St. Giles Cathedral in Edinburgh, when Jenny Geddes threw her stool at the minister, denouncing bishops in the Kirk.

The clan motto is *Nunquam non paratus* — "Never unprepared". The badge is a winged spur.

TARTAN The Johnstone tartan has a green background with black checks and yellow stripes. Septs include Marchbanks and Rome.

The romantic ruins of mighty Dunnottar Castle, standing on a great headland near Stonehaven, Kincardine, symbolize the dramatic part the Keiths, who held the office of Great Marischal (Marshall) of Scotland for nearly 700 years, played in the turbulent past. The Scottish regalia, the Crown, Sceptre and Sword, and the state papers were brought here for safety when Oliver Cromwell invaded Scotland. After he defeated Charles II, Dunnottar was the last Scottish stronghold still flying the Royal Standard. It held out for eight months but finally surrendered on 24 May, 1652. However, the English victors were cheated of the most important of their spoils. The Scottish regalia were lowered down the walls to an old woman gathering seaweed on the shore. She carried them hidden in her creel to the nearby Kineff Church where they were hidden in the pulpit until the restoration of the monarchy.

The Keiths are probably descended from ancient Celtic stock. First to be mentioned is Hervey Keith, who was Marischal in the 12th-century reign of Malcolm IV. By the time of Robert the Bruce, Keith had been granted the royal forest of Kintore, Aberdeenshire, and his command of the cavalry at the Battle of Bannockburn in 1314 helped to win the day.

The hereditary office was made into an Earldom in 1458, when the 2nd Lord became Earl Marischal. The 2nd Earl, whose standard is still preserved in Edinburgh, fought at Flodden in 1513. By the time of the 3rd Earl, a scholarly recluse, the estates were so vast that he could travel from Berwick in the South to John o'Groats in the furthest North on his own lands.

The 4th Earl entertained Mary, Queen of Scots, at Dunnottar Castle. Her son, James VI, in a Privy Council held there, appointed the 5th Earl Marischal to stand proxy for him at his marriage to Anne of Denmark. George, the last Earl Marischal, who died in 1788, and his brother, James, were both ardent Jacobites. The estates forfeited, they fled to the Continent, where James was made a Field Marshall by Frederick the Great before dying in battle in 1758. With the end of the line of hereditary Marischals, the Earl of Kintore, a descendant of the younger Keith son who helped to save the Scottish regalia, is now the head of the Keiths.

The clan motto is *Veritas vincit* — "Truth conquers". The badge is a ten-pointer stag's head.

TARTAN The clan tartan is usually called the Keith and Austin tartan (the Austins are a sept of the clan) and is an old design of greens and blues. Septs include Dickson, Falconer, Harvey, Hurrie, Lumgair, Marshall, and Urie.

Though the clan Kennedy has several interesting American connections, it is not thought to originate from Ireland, like the late President Kennedy's family, but from the Celtic lords of Galloway, that far south-western peninsula which is the nearest crossing point to Ireland.

Like the Irish Kennedys, the Scottish clan have close links with the United States. The clan chiefs, the Earls of Cassilis, at one time owned a substantial part of New York City, while after World War II General Eisenhower was given a apartment for his permanent use in the magnificent Culzean Castle. Built for the 10th Earl of Cassilis by Robert Adam in the 18th century, on a site associated with the Kennedys for hundreds of years, the castle now has an Eisenhower room dedicated to the General's career.

The Kennedys dominated all the south-west of Scotland, from Wigtownshire up to Ayrshire, even before John Kennedy of Dunure and Cassilis married the heiress of the Carrick Earls. Their grandson strengthened their power in the 15th century by marrying the daughter of King Robert III and was made Lord Kennedy. His younger brother became one of Scotland's most important medieval churchmen. As Bishop of St. Andrews, he founded St. Salvator's College and acted as an adviser to King James II throughout his reign. When the King was accidentally killed by a cannon in 1460, the Bishop advised his widow on the education of the young James III. After the powerful prelate's death in 1465 there was a palace revolution in which the Boyds, aided by the Bishop's brother, Lord Kennedy, held power as regents until the King came of age.

But it was not until James IV's reign that the 3rd Lord Kennedy, soon to die with his King on the battlefield of Flodden, was made Earl of Cassilis. Later Earls were more ruthless in their quest for land and power. The 4th Earl of Cassilis was notorious for having roasted the Abbot of Crossraguel over a slow fire in his castle of Dunure to force him to surrender the titles to the abbey properties. The Abbot survived, but the Earl got what he wanted.

Just as merciless was the 17th-century 6th Earl, whose wife fell in love with Johnnie Faa, the gypsy king whose ancestors had been granted the right to rule their tribe by James V in 1540. The ballad of Johnnie Faa describes how she "threw off her gay mantle for a plaid so that she could follow the gypsy laddie". But the Earl caught up with the eloping lovers, hanged Johnnie Faa before the Countess' eyes, and imprisoned her in his Castle of Cassilis for the rest of her life.

Archibald, the 11th Earl, was a naval officer who fought in the American War of Independence but still found time to buy some prime real estate in New York. His son, the 12th Earl, was created the Marquis of Ailsa in 1806, taking the title from the rock in the Firth of Clyde, Ailsa Craig, within view from his sumptuous new Castle of Culzean.

The present chief, Archibald, the 7th Marquess of Ailsa, whose heir is the Earl of Cassilis, lives at Cassilis House, Maybole, in Ayrshire.

The clan motto is *Avise la fin* — "Consider the end". The badge is a dolphin.

TARTAN The distinctive Kennedy tartan has yellow and purple stripes against a green background.

This clan name, with several forms, such as Kerr, Ker and Carr, is traditionally said to be of Norman origin, deriving from two brothers, John and Ralph Ker, who settled in Roxburgh in the Scottish Borders in the 14th century. The chief of the clan, the 12th Marquess of Lothian, still lives in Roxburghshire at Monteviot, near Ancrum.

The two branches of the family, the Kers of Ferniehurst, descendants of the elder brother Ralph, and the Kers of Cessford, ended up feuding with each other. Though at the beginning of the 16th century the keeping of the Middle March of the Borders was divided between them, each taking office alternately, their own constant rivalry was not conducive to maintaining law and order. Their two castles were only six miles apart and not much further from the English border. The Castle of Cessford is now an impressive ruin near Morebattle, on the north edge of the Cheviots, while Ferniehurst Castle, acquired through marriage, has been superseded as a Ker residence by a newer building, though it remains a clan possession.

The phrase "Jeddart justice" is said to have come from the Kerrs' way of dealing with their enemies. Jeddart justice entailed putting someone to death and then trying him afterwards, or as novelist Sir Walter Scott more succinctly put it, "hang in haste and try at leisure". True to form, the two sides supported different royal factions, the Cessford family aiding the pro-English party of Margaret Tudor, widow of James IV, while the Ferniehurst faction backed James V.

Unlike Shakespeare's Montagues and Capulets, love finally conquered all when the two sides were united in marriage. The Marquesses of Lothian are descended from the marriage of Anne Kerr of Cessford to William Kerr of Ferniehurst in 1631, after which the Earldom of Lothian was created.

From the Cessford line of Kerrs came another title, that of Lord Roxburghe which later, in 1707, became the Dukedom of Roxburghe, the title afterwards to be inherited by the Innes clan of which the Duke is now the chief. The splendid Kerr buildings, Floors Castle, home of the Roxburghes, and Newbattle Abbey, near Edinburgh, which the 11th Marquess of Lothian handed over to an adult education residential college, are stone monuments to the wealth of the Kerrs.

The clan motto is *Sero sed serio* — "Late but in earnest". The badge is a shining sun.

TARTAN The Kerr tartan, green and black checks on a red background, is rather similar to that of Stewart of Atholl, though there is no connection between them.

The clan Lamont — or Lamond — is one of the most ancient of the Scottish clans with a well-documented genealogy, but, as its historian points out, it is a clan which has had a capacity for emigration. For most of this century the chiefs have lived in Australia, the home of the present 28th Lamont of Lamont.

The Lamonts came to Scotland from Ireland to help found the Kingdom of Dalriada, one of whose districts, now the modern Cowal in Argyllshire, was named after King Comgall, killed in 537. Like St. Columba, the Lamonts are descended from this royal house of O'Neill.

The first Lamont chief on record in 1200 is Ferchar, whose sons gave lands at Kilmun, beside the Holy Loch (now the site of the American Polaris submarine base), and the church of Kilfinan to the monks of Paisley. The clan's name comes from Lauman, the grandson of Ferchar. Toward Castle, now a magnificent ruin near Dunoon commanding a wide sweep of the Firth of Clyde, was the clan seat when they owned most of Cowal and entertained Mary, Queen of Scots, there in 1563.

The Lamonts consistently supported the losing side. They opposed Robert the Bruce, and Charles I's attempt to introduce the episcopalian liturgy. After Montrose was defeated, the Campbells of Argyll, Lamont's powerful neighbours, ravaged the clan lands, besieging and destroying Sir James Lamont's Toward Castle in 1646. They took 200 prisoners to Dunoon and massacred them at Gallowhill, with 36 of the "special gentlemen" of the clan hanged on a single tree. The Clan Lamont Society, founded in 1895, put up a memorial on this site in 1906. The mainline of Lamonts died out in 1929, and the succession passed to the cadet branch whose heir had emigrated to Australia.

With financial help from America, a history was published in 1938 by the Clan Lamont Society. The 15th-century Lamont clarsach (a small harp), the oldest surviving example of Scotland's ancient musical instrument, is now in the Royal Museum of Scotland in Edinburgh.

There are many clan septs, including Black, Brown, Clement, Douglas, Forsyth, Lamb, Lucas, MacClymont, MacFarquhar, Mackerchar, Maclemon, MacMunn, MacPatrick, MacSorley, Paterson, Patrick, Toward, Turner and White.

The clan motto is *Ne parcas nec spernas* — "Neither spare nor dispose". The badge is a raised hand.

TARTAN The Lamont tartan is similar to the Campbell of Argyll tartan, except that it has no yellow stripes.

The chief of the Leslie clan is the 21st Earl of Rothes, who lives at West Tytherley, Salisbury, Wiltshire. The clan originated in Aberdeenshire when a Flemish nobleman, Bartholf, settled on the lands of Leslie behind Bennachie in the 12th century. The clan has had its up and downs, prudently surviving the fall of the neighbouring Comyns, but suffering from "a chronic and adventurous poverty" as one historian put it. Their fame was won latterly as soldiers of fortune rather than as influential landowners.

Although they made royal marriages and became the Earls of Ross before the end of the 14th century, that title became the cause of a battle royal when the Earl of Ross died in 1402 and his only child became a nun. At the Battle of Harelaw in 1411, where six sons of Leslie of Balquhain are said to have been killed, Donald of the Isles fought and won the title, only for it to be lost again when the power of the Lord of the Isles was broken.

Before that, Sir Andrew Leslie had been made Earl of Rothes in 1467 by James II. The 3rd Earl died at Flodden and the 4th Earl accompanied James V to France and died at Dieppe. The 7th Earl carried the sword of state at Charles II's coronation at Scone in 1651 and was made Duke of Rothes in 1680, but again when he died in 1681 he left only a daughter, whose elder son became the 8th Earl of Rothes.

But it was as military men that the Leslies gained the greatest honours. At one point in the 17th century there were three Leslie generals serving in three different countries. Sir Alexander Leslie, the 1st Earl of Leven (a title now united with that of the Melvilles) was a famous Scottish general during the civil war, having previously been made a field-marshal by the King of Sweden. Sir Alexander of Auchintoul became a general in Russia, while Walter Leslie, of the Balquhain branch, fought in Germany, along with other Leslie soldiers of lower ranks, and was made a Count.

Besides the Earldom of Rothes, other branches of the Leslie clan have been honoured with the peerages of Newark, Leven and Lindores. From the senior branch of Balquhain came Count Leslie, who assassinated Wallenstein, and the Baronets of Wardis and of Warthill.

The clan motto is "Grip fast" and the badge a half-griffon.

TARTAN There are three Leslie tartans, dress, hunting and red. The hunting tartan, shown here, is older and darker. The dress tartan may be a variant of the dress Brodie. Septs are Abernethy, Lesslie and More.

Chief of the clan Lindsay is the 29th Earl of Crawford and Balcarres, of Pitcorthie, Colinsburgh, Fife, the Premier Earl of Scotland. His dual titles carry the history of two prominent lines of Lindsay, "ane surname of renown" as a literary Lindsay, Sir David of the Mount, a 16th-century Lord Lyon King of arms, wrote. He was the author of the drama, *The Three Estaits*, a bold satire on the need for reformation, which has been performed at several Edinburgh Festivals.

The Lindsays came to Scotland from Lincolnshire with David I in the 12th century and settled on the lands of Crawford, Lanarkshire. In 1340 Sir David Lindsay acquired Glenesk in Angus through marriage to an heiress of the Earl of Angus,1 an area in which the clan expanded and prospered.

The Crawford line produced some dramatic characters. The 4th Earl, who became known as "Tiger Earl" or "Beardie Earl", ruled over a vast community of vassals but allied himself with the Douglases in a rebellion against James II, and had to plead for mercy. Stranger still was "the Wicked Master", Alexander, heir to the 8th Earl, who was convicted of trying to kill his father and was disinherited. The title passed to his cousin, the Laird of Edzell, although it reverted to the original line when the 9th Earl died.

The Laird of Edzell's great-grandson was made Earl of Balcarres in 1651, which led eventually the union of the two great houses in 1808. The 6th Earl of Balcarres then also became the 23rd Earl of Crawford when the direct Lindsay line failed.

Considered a clannish people, the Lindsays also had a reputation for liveliness, being known as the "Lightsome Lindsays". They were one of the few Lowland clans to set up their own Clan Association, which they did in 1897 under their clan chief, with headquarters in Edinburgh and a branch in Glasgow. To establish their 19th-century claim to the Earldom of Crawford the chief's son researched the family history and published the results in a book called *The Lives of the Lindsays*.

Recent chiefs have contributed greatly to preserving Britain's heritage. The 28th Chief, father of the present Earl, was a trustee of the British Museum and the National and the Tate Galleries, as well as being involved with the National Trust and the Pilgrim Trust. The 29th chief is chairman of Scotland's Historic Buildings Council.

The clan motto is *Endure fort* — "Endure with strength". The badge is a swan rising out of a coronet.

TARTAN The Lindsay tartan is a variation of that of Stewart of Atholl, with the black checks being replaced by blue ones.

The MacAlisters are one of the chief branches of the clan Donald. The founder was Alasdair Mor, younger son of Donald, originator of the clan Donald, and grandson of Somerled of Argyll. He is mentioned in Irish records as having been killed in 1299 in a fight with his cousin, Alasdair MacDougall of the senior line of Somerled.

Never a very numerous clan, the MacAlisters had lands in South Knapdale, Kintyre. The ancient seat of the chief lies north of West Loch Tarbert. Charles MacAlister was appointed to the stewartry of Kintyre in 1481 by James III. But it was Charles' son, John of the Loup (from the Gaelic meaning bend or creek in the shore), with his lands on the south shore of West Loch Tarbert, after whom later chiefs were named.

In the 15th and 16th centuries, the clan also spread into the islands of Bute and Arran in the Firth of Clyde, where their descendants live to this day. Another branch of the clan MacAlister became hereditary keepers of the royal castle of Tarbert, strategically placed on the isthmus between Kintyre and Knapdale.

Alexander (the English form of the Gaelic name Alasdair) of the Loup fought for James VII at the battle of Killiecrankie and, escaping to Ireland with the remains of his followers, fought at the Battle of the Boyne with the Royalists against William of Orange.

After the '45 the MacAlisters of Tarbert were bankrupt and had to sell their castle and lands. But in the 18th century Charles, the 12th chief of Loup, married the wealthy heiress of Somerville of Kennox, Ayrshire, and the chiefs of MacAlister have lived there ever since.

The clan motto is *Fortiter* — "Boldly". The badge is a hand holding a dagger.

TARTAN This MacAlister tartan, the older of the two, is complex and can be recognized as belonging to the group of MacDonald tartans. The second tartan omits the white and light green lines and has links with the MacDougall patterns.

Septs include Allison, MacAlaster, MacAllister, Sanders and Saunders.

Siol Alpin is the name given to a number of clans, widely separated — unlike that other clan confederation, clan Chattan — but all supposed to have royal connections, being descended from Kenneth MacAlpine, the ancestor of the long line of Scottish Kings.

These clans include the Gregors, Grants, Mackinnons, Macquarries, MacNabs and MacAulays, all claiming to be the most ancient and noble of Highland clans. King Alpin of Dalriada, the son of Kenneth, was murdered in 834.

There is little historical evidence about the clan MacAlpine. Their traditional seat was said to be Dunstaffnage, Argyllshire. The family of the chief is not known, the clan is landless, and it has no crest or badge.

TARTAN The tartan called MacAlpine is the same as the hunting Maclean, apart from the fact that the white lines have been changed to yellow. It has a green background, unlike all the other tartans of the *Siol Alpin*, which have a red one.

Mythology has it that the MacArthurs are descended from the legendary King Arthur, that early British resistance fighter who may have fought the Scots and the Picts for his southern Scottish kingdom before his heroic exploits were recorded in the Welsh language.

But what certainly is true is that the MacArthurs are one of the most ancient clans of Argyllshire, with lands on the shores of Loch Awe. Their war-cry is *Eisd! O Eisd!* which means "Listen! O Listen!", and an ancient Gaelic couplet enforces their antiquity: "There is nothing older, unless the hills, McArthur and the devil".

The clan is thought to be an older branch of the clan Campbell and to have held that chiefship in earlier centuries. But in 1427 Iain MacArthur, as one of the leading chiefs in Argyll, was executed by James I on his return from captivity in England and his lands forfeited, a disaster from which the clan MacArthur never recovered.

It has been left to clan descendants to bring fame to the name overseas, particularly in Australia and America. John MacArthur, an 18th-century descendant of the MacArthurs of Strachur, the principal branch of the clan, is honoured as the "father" of New South Wales. He arrived there in 1790 with his regiment and became commandant at Parramatta from 1793 to 1804. To him the Australian wool trade owes its beginnings, since he was the first to cross the Bengal with the Irish sheep and to introduce Merino sheep from Africa. In 1817, he planted the first vineyard, the start of the Australian wine-making industry.

A modern MacArthur won fame in America, to which his grandfather had emigrated from Strathclyde in 1840. He was General Douglas MacArthur, the conqueror of Japan in World War II.

The clan slogan is *Fide et opera* — "By fidelity and work". The badge is two laurel wreaths.

TARTAN Though a clan of Campbell stock, the MacArthurs also had links with the MacDonalds — the MacArthurs of Skye were hereditary pipers to the MacDonalds of the Isles — and their tartan has the same basic form as that of the Lord of the Isles. It also has similarities with the hunting version of the MacIver, who also lived in Campbell country.
Septs include Arthur, Dewar, Maccairter and Macindeor.

The MacAulays are a branch of the clan Alpin, but there are two completely separate clans of MacAulays. The first clan is said to take its name from Aulay, younger son of Alwin, Earl of Lennox, with lands at Ardencaple on the Gareloch in lowland Dunbartonshire. The second clan, the MacAulays of Lewis in the outer Hebrides, claims descent from a Norseman called Olaf.

The MacAulays of Ardencaple owned their lands from Cardross to Garelochhead for nearly five centuries. But by the end of the 16th century they were acknowledging that they were a cadet clan of the MacGregors, and by 1594 they joined the MacGregors in a roll of the broken clans. However they did manage to retain their castle and lands of Ardencaple until the last chief died in 1767, when they were sold to the Campbells of Argyll to pay debts. The modern town of Helensburgh and the Trident submarine base at Faslane are now on the old MacAulay lands.

The MacAulays of Lewis had lands at Uig, in the southwest of the island. They are said to be descended from Aula or Olaf the Black, brother of Magnus, last King of Man and the Isles, and were probably followers of the MacLeods of Lewis. The 19th-century historian, Lord Macaulay, was a descendant of the Lewis clan.

The clan motto is *Dulce periculum* — "Danger is sweet". The badge is a spurred riding boot.

TARTAN There are three MacAulay tartans, two of which are very similar with green checks on a red background. This darker green is the modern hunting tartan. Septs of either clan include Aulay, Macalley and Maccauley.

An American businessman, Hughston McBain of McBain, was recognized as chief of the clan by the Lord Lyon King of Arms in 1959. Since then the chief has established a memorial park near the clan heartland at Kinchyle, Dores, Loch Ness, from where his own ancestors came.

Three different Gaelic names are suggested as the origin of the clan name, since corrupted into English, and giving the various forms of MacBean, MacBain and even McVean. *Mac A'Ghille Bhain* means "the son of the fair lad", *Mac Maol Bheatha* is "the son of the servant of life", whilst the third alternative is *Mac Beathain*, "the son of Beathan".

The MacBeans were traditionally said to be among the most loyal supporters of the clan Chattan, with lands in Lochaber. According to the legends of the Mackintoshes, a father and his four MacBean sons placed themselves under Mackintosh protection after slaying the steward of the Red Comyn.

MacBean chiefs can be traced from the 14th century down to 1609, when Angus MacBean, the chief, received the charter of Kinchyle from Campbell of Cawdor, which they held until the 18th century. The MacBeans were warriors and one of the most famous was Gillies MacBean, who filled a breach in the lines at Culloden, killing 14 Hanoverians before he fell. The next chief, who was in financial difficulties, joined one of the first Highland regiments and served in North America. In his absence, Kinchyle and other lands had to be sold in 1760.

The main clan line had by then moved overseas to Saskatchewan, represented by MacBean of Glen Bean, who in 1958 resigned his chiefship in favour of his American cousin. Other branches of the clan were the MacBeans of Drummond in the parish of Dores, MacBean of Faillie in Strathnairn and Mac-Bean of Tomatin in Strathdearn.

Beaton, a distinguished Highland name, is another anglicized form of the Gaelic *MacBeatha*. This family, said to come originally from Ireland after Margaret, daughter of O'Cathain married Angus, Lord of the Isles, had the most advanced European medical knowledge in the 13th century. They were physicians and scholars in the Isles, but the last scholar fled back to Northern Ireland in the 17th century, taking his great manuscript library with him, when he was asked to conform to the Presbyterian faith.

TARTAN The ancient MacBean tartan is considered by the experts to be curiously elaborate for what was only a minor sept of the clan Chattan. Septs include Binni, MacBeath, MacBeth, Macvain and MacVean.

MacCallum means a follower of St. Columba. His name in Gaelic was Colm and he was distinguished from others of the same name by adding a suffix, *Columchille*. The Gaelic *Maol Caluim* means "devotee of Columba" and the history of this clan is inextricably mixed with the other form of the name, Malcolm. Indeed, the chief of the clan is the 18th Laird of Poltalloch, Robin Malcolm, who still lives in the ancient castle of Duntrune, near Lochgilphead, Argyllshire from which their 16th-century charter derives.

In the 15th century, the chief of the Campbells granted lands to Reginald MacCallum of Corbarron in Craignish on the banks of Loch Avich, Argyllshire, along with the hereditary keepership of the Castles of Lochaffy and Craignish. The last of that family left Corbarron to Zachary MacCallum of Poltalloch. Dugald MacCallum of Poltalloch, who succeded to the title in 1779, was the first to start using the name Malcolm. The 15th Laird was created Lord Malcolm of Poltalloch in 1896 but died without an heir in 1902, being succeeded by his brother.

The clan motto is *In ardua petit*— "He has attempted difficult things" — though the clan also had an old motto *Deus refugiam nostrum* — "God is our refuge". The badge is a castle.

TARTAN There are two MacCallum tartans. The ancient MaCallum tartan, shown here, has been supplanted by the more modern one. There is also a Malcolm tartan, which is not thought to be of ancient origin since it is asymetrical, breaking the common custom of weaving tartan.

Septs of the clan include Callam and Callum.

The mighty MacDonalds, the most powerful, widespread and ancient of all the Highland clans, ruled the Highlands as the Lords of the Isles for nearly four centuries, threatening at one time to command the Kingdom of Scotland itself. They entered into the Treaty of Ardtornish with the King of England in 1462, dividing up Scotland into Gaelic- and English-speaking halves. The Gaelic half was to be ruled by the MacDonalds and the English-speaking Lowlands by the Douglases if the English defeated the Stewart King James III. But by the end of the century John, 4th and last Lord of the Isles, had been stripped of his possessions and his title. After his downfall, anarchy reigned in the Highlands and Islands and the poets lamented: "It is no joy without the clan Donald. It is no strength to be without them."

The blood brotherhood of the MacDonalds, descendants of Somerled, who defeated the Norse rulers of the Isles, and the unswerving loyalty of the other clans in their Highland confederation — such as the Macleans, Macleods, Macneils, Mackinnons, Macquarries and Macfies — was their great strength. But the Lord of the Isles' downfall also split up the powerful clan structure so devastatingly that, even by the end of the 16th century, no one leader had emerged to take control over what had become by then nine or more different branches. By the mid-17th century, three MacDonald chieftains, Sir James of Sleat, the Captain of Clanranald and Lord MacDonell of Glengarry, were ordered to try and keep the peace in the Highlands. But as late as the beginning of this century the successors of these three titles were ignominiously tossing a coin to decide who should take precedence.

Finally, in 1947, the Lord Lyon King of Arms ruled that the Baronet of Sleat should be allowed to use the title 'MacDonald of MacDonald' and restored to him the arms of the chief of the MacDonalds. Ironically, this Lordship of the House of Sleat *(Clann Huistean)* is an Irish peerage, granted in 1776 to the 9th Laird of Sleat. This Irish enoblement was a cunning way to prevent Scots from having the right to sit in the House of Lords, since Irish peers have no such right. The Sleat estates were split between two brothers in the 19th century so that one could succeed to the Bosville Yorkshire estates of a great-grandmother, while the other brother kept the MacDonald title and Scottish lands.

The present chief of the clan MacDonald, Godfrey, 8th Baron MacDonald, still lives on Skye, at Ostaig House. He and his wife, Lady Claire, a leading food expert and cookery writer, run a hotel not far from Armadale Castle, which is now the clan Mac-

Donald centre. Sir Ian Bosville MacDonald of Sleat, the 25th chief of Sleat, is head of this branch of the clan, and lives at Thorpe Hall, Driffield, Yorkshire.

The MacDonalds also claim to be of Irish origin. Descent from Colla Uais, High King of Ireland, is one claim made for them. Their descent is authentically recorded from Somerled, son of Gillebride, who arrived in Morvern in obscure circumstances about the end of the 10th century. The Norse hold on the western mainland and Isles was then beginning to weaken and Somerled successfully evicted them from Lochaber, Morvern and North Argyll, later, in a sea battle, defeating Godfrey, King of Man. After forays against the Gaels of Ireland and the King, Malcolm IV, Somerled was killed in battle in 1164.

He left three sons, Dugald, Reginald (or Ranald) and Angus, among whom his Kingdom was divided, thus setting up the great branch lines of the future clan MacDonald. It was Reginald's son, Donald of Islay, who inherited that island plus Kintyre and gave the clan its name. During the Wars of Independence Alexander, chief of the clan, opposed Bruce, while his brother, Angus Og, supported him, and ended up with the clan lands. Thereafter he ruled the Isles like an independent King. A later Lord of the Isles, John, married the daughter of King Robert II, which led eventually to the battle of Harlaw in 1411 when the MacDonalds fought for, and finally won, the title of Earl of Ross. However, James I had twice imprisoned Alasdair of the Isles, the great Highland potentate, once in Inverness and a second time after he had rebelled on release and been defeated in Tantallon Castle, when he went to seek pardon in Edinburgh. This time his clansmen rose in revolt and he was released.

It was Alasdair's son, John, who, declaring his kingdom independent, entered into the Ardtornish treaty with England, and eventually was stripped of all his titles and possessions, ending the proud dynasty of the Lord of the Isles. Thereafter the main branches of the clan, like the MacDonalds of Clanranald, the Macdonalds of Sleat, and the Macdonnells of Glengarry, went their separate ways, making their own contributions to the history of Scotland.

The clan motto is *Per mare per terras* — "By sea and by land". The badge is a clenched, armoured hand holding a cross.

TARTAN There are 14 different MacDonald tartans. The red-and-green design (above left) is the comprehensive one. The Lord of the Isles hunting tartan (above right) is unlike any other, yet is recognizable as a MacDonald tartan.

· MACDONALD ·
OF CLANRANALD

Chief of this branch of the clan Donald is Ranald Macdonald, Captain of Clanranald, whose business address is 74 Upper Street, Islington, London. The clan takes its name from Ranald, younger son of John Lord of the Isles, by his first marriage to Amy McRuari (or McRory), who succeeded to his mother's estates.

It was Clanranald's son who got Alasdair, Lord of the Isles, freed from Tantallon Castle by invading Lochaber and losing his own life. But Dugald, the 6th chief, was so vicious a character that he was murdered by his own kinsmen and succeeded by his uncle, Alistair. Alistair's natural son, John of Moidart, had the title conferred on himself in 1530 at the family stronghold of Castle Tirrim (now in ruins on an islet in Loch Moidart) but was imprisoned 10 years later by James V for his unruly conduct.

While he was out of circulation, an unsuccessful attempt was made to replace him by a son of the 5th chief, which led to the battle known as *Blar-Na-Leine* (the field of the shirts) because the fighters threw off their plaids and skirmished clad only in long shirts.

Clanranald went to war again to support Montrose, with 16-year-old John, the 11th chief, leading 500 clansmen into battle at Killiecrankie. Alexander, the 13th chief, was killed at the Battle of Sheriffmuir, to be succeeded by his brother, Ranald, who died at the Jacobite court in France.

Bonnie Prince Charlie raised his standard on Clanranald land and "young Clanranald", later the 17th chief, was one of his most fervent supporters. After Culloden, the Prince took refuge in Clanranald lands in Benbecula and Uist before sailing for France, while the chief had to go into exile after barely escaping with his life.

In the 19th century, the chief who inherited the 500-year-old estates which were worth a fortune frittered most of it away in Regency London and Brighton, while rents were being squeezed out of his tenants. From 1828 his lands were sold off to the Gordons, one of the most ruthless exponents of the Highland Clearances.

After the 23rd chief died without issue in 1944, the Lord Lyon was asked to decide between the competing claims of the septs of Boisdale and Waternish, deciding in favour of Boisdale, making Ranald MacDonald 24th Chief of Clanranald.

The clan motto is "My hope is constant in thee" and the badge is a castle surmounted by an armoured arm holding a sword.

TARTAN The Clanranald tartan is similar to the Macdonald with the addition of two white lines. Again, there are many septs of this clan.

· M A C D O N E L L ·
OF GLENGARRY

In Ontario, Canada, there is a county called after the men of Glengarry, who joined the regiment raised by Duncan, their 14th chief, at the end of the 18th century. After it was disbanded in 1801 most of the men, still Gaelic speakers, emigrated to Canada, where they founded a settlement on the banks of the St. Lawrence.

Perhaps it was as well that they emigrated, for their 15th chief, Alasdair, became a walking parody of a Highland chieftain at the expense of his clansmen. Accoutred in the panoply of Highland dress on all occasions, with a retinue of retainers also in full Highland costume, this flamboyant figure had his portrait painted by Raeburn and moved in the Edinburgh literary circles of Walter Scott. Meanwhile in his vast lands, his destitute clansmen were having to leave. These included the next chief, Aeneas, who had to sell off debt-ridden estates, inherited from his father in 1828, and, with his sons, emigrate to Australia and later New Zealand.

Although it sounds Irish, the MacDonell spelling comes from the Gaelic *MacDhomhnuill*, which this branch of the Macdonalds chose as being nearer their original name. MacDonnell of Glengarry is a cadet branch of Clanranald, which in turn was descended from a younger son of the Lord of the Isles. A MacDonell chief married the heiress of Sir Alexander Macdonald of Lochalsh, which brought a charter to the castle of Strome but also a bitter feud. The MacDonells claimed that this marriage made them rightful heirs to the whole clan MacDonald, but the MacKenzies also claimed the Lochalsh lands, which led to many bloody battles.

In 1672, Donald, the 8th chief, was made a Baronet, while his son, Angus, was created Lord MacDonnell and Aros, a peerage which expired with him in 1680. Alastair, the 11th chief, carried the royal standard of James VII in 1689 at Killiecrankie and the clan mustered 500 armed clansmen in 1745.

A younger son of Duncan, the 14th chief who raised the Highland regiment in 1794, became General Sir James MacDonell, who was praised by Wellington for his conduct at Waterloo, and became Governor-General of Canada in 1838.

Air Commodore Donald MacDonell of Glengarry, of Fortrose, Ross-shire, now represents the clan MacDonell.

The clan motto is the same as its war cry, *Creagan an Fhithich*, which means "the raven's rock". Its badge is a raven perched on a rock.

TARTAN The MacDonell of Glengarry is the same as the MacDonald tartan, with the addition of a white line.

· M A C D O N A L D ·
OF SLEAT

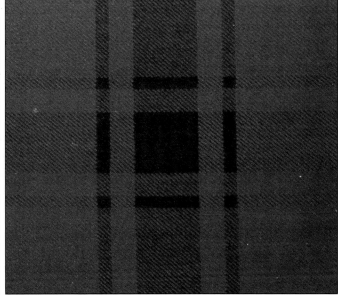

The MacDonalds of Sleat, a parish on Skye containing the sites of three MacDonald castles, Dunskaith, Camus and Armadale, are of particular importance in the history of the clan Donald. They were the heirs of the last Earl of Ross and Lord of the Isles, and it is from their line that the MacDonald of Macdonald, chief of the whole clan, now comes.

They are descended from Hugh, son of Alasdair, Lord of the Isles, which is why they are often called *Clann Huistean*, meaning "children of Hugh". Alternatively, they are called clan Donald North, to distinguish them from the MacDonalds of Islay. Hugh died at Sleat just after his brother John, last Lord of the Isles, had his title forfeited in 1493.

The next six chiefs of Sleat, whose seat was the castle of Dunskaith, were all called Donald. Donald Gallach, so called because he married Elizabeth Gunn, daughter of the famous Coroner of Caithness, was murdered by a half-brother in 1506. The former's son, Donald Grumach, meaning "Grim", died in 1534 and his son, Donald Gorm, died in 1539, killed by an arrow shot by a MacRae defender as he besieged Eilean Donan Castle in a vain attempt to restore the title of Lord of the Isles. His son, Donald, was known as *Domnhull Gorm Sasunnach* because he had spent his youth in England. Donald Gorm Mor came to terms with James VI in 1596 and received the charter to lands at Trotternish and also led 500 of his clansmen to help the Irish rebels in their fight against the English crown, though, a year or two later, he offered his services to the Queen Elizabeth.

The sixth Donald became a Baronet in 1625, one of the earliest Baronets of Nova Scotia, with some 16,000 acres to his name in New Brunswick. He died in 1643, shortly before a large body of his clansmen joined the royalist, Montrose. The 3rd Baronet sent 500 men to fight for James VII at Killiecrankie and the title was forfeited but later restored.

In 1776 the 9th Baronet was created Lord MacDonald in the peerage of Ireland. In 1832 when Godfrey, the 3rd Lord MacDonald died, Alexander, his heir, took the name of Bosville to succeed to the Yorkshire inheritance while his brother took the MacDonald lordship. In 1910 Sir Alexander resumed the MacDonald name, becoming Bosville MacDonald of Sleat, and his descendant, Sir Ian, of Thorpe Hall, Driffield, Yorkshire, is now 25th chief of Sleat.

TARTAN This MacDonald of Sleat tartan was manufactured in the 18th century and called MacDonald of Sleat, Lord of the Isles, but this is said to be a defective rendering of the old MacDonald tartan shown in a painting at Armadale Castle.

· MACDOUGALL ·

· MACDUFF ·

Like the MacDonalds, the clan MacDougall is descended from the sons of Somerled's marriage to Ragnhild, Norse sister of Godfrey, King of Man. In their case the eldest son, Dougal, who was the senior heir of the Gaelic-Norse stock, was the founder of the clan. The lands of Lorn, heartland of the clan, were given by Dougal to his son, Duncan, to which were added the islands of Mull, Coll and Tiree. Some of the 10 great castles they are said to have built included Dunstaffnage, Dunollie and the island fortresses of Cairnburg on the Treshnish isles and Dunchonnel on the Garvellach islands.

Madam MacDougall of MacDougall, who succeeded her father (her husband changed his name to MacDougall) in 1953, is the 29th chief of the clan, and although the ancient Castle of Dunollie at Oban, Argyllshire, is now in ruins, she still lives beside it. The eldest unmarried daughter of the chief has the old title of "Maid of Lorn".

Ewen, son of Duncan, had to surrender the islands to the Norwegian King when he arrived with his fleet in 1263, later to be defeated in the sea battle off Largs, and threw in his lot with the Scottish King Alexander III. Ewen's son, Alasdair, having married a sister of the Red Comyn, became involved in a bitter feud with Bruce. This is how the clan gained its proudest possession, the Brooch of Lorn, the pin from Bruce's cloak, which he discarded as he fled defeated from an encounter with the MacDougalls in the Pass of Brander by Loch Awe. Bruce had his revenge when he became King and dispossessed the MacDougalls of their islands for all time. However they managed to get back the lordship of Lorne in 1344 after Ewen, the 5th MacDougall chief, married, Bruce's grand-daughter, Joanna MacIsaak. He had no sons, and after his death, the estates passed to the Stewarts of Innermeath, two brothers who had married Ewen's two daughters. The chiefship passed to the daughters' cousin, Ian MacDougall, who became the 7th chief.

In 1457 Sir John MacDougall, the 10th chief, managed to get a charter of Kerrara and Dunollie, and these Dunollie lands stayed in the family until they were forfeited in 1715, when the 21st chief went with 200 clansmen to the Battle of Sheriffmuir.

The clan motto is *Buaidh no bas* which means "to conquer or die". The badge is an arm in armour holding a cross.

TARTAN This is one of the four versions of the MacDougall tartan, which has a red background with multiple stripes. The variety seems to be due to confusion by manufacturers in the 19th century as to the exact pattern. There are a great many septs of this clan.

The MacDuffs are of the most ancient royal stock in Scotland, descendants of the Scottish-Pictish royal house. Queen Gruoch, translated by Shakespeare into Lady Macbeth, was the head of that line. Her second husband, King Macbeth, was also said to belong to the house of Duff, but it was Malcolm Canmore who, with English help, won power and whose sons gained the Scottish throne.

The Celtic Earl of Fife, traditionally the great MacDuff, may well have helped Canmore to overthrow Macbeth. As a friend of the new King, he had an Earldom from 1107 as well as being Abbot of Dunkeld, the ancient Perthshire town whose name comes from *Dun Chailleann*, meaning "the fort of the Caledonians". The MacDuffs held their territories by grace of God in the Celtic style, rather than from the King, which some suggest is the reason why the region of Fife is still known as a Kingdom today.

This powerful family had very special privileges. These included the right of the clan MacDuff to crown the Scottish kings, to lead the Scottish army, and to have sanctuary, if accused of homicide, at the cross of MacDuff, north of Newburgh, Fife. When Robert the Bruce, after the Wars of Independence against English domination, was crowned King at Scone in 1306, the Earl of Fife, who had married a niece of the English King Edward I, was, not unnaturally, absent from the occasion. But his sister, Isabel, Countess of Buchan, who was also married to one of Bruce's enemies, John Comyn, still bravely performed her family's function of placing the crown on Bruce's head. Not long afterwards she was taken prisoner by Edward I and imprisoned in a cage suspended from the walls of Berwick Castle, where she remained for seven long years.

In 1353 Duncan, the 11th Earl of Fife, died leaving an only daughter and the Earldom became extinct, though in 1757 the Lord Lyon declared the Earl of Wemyss as the representative of the MacDuffs. The present Duke of Fife, the 3rd titleholder, who is also the Earl of MacDuff, is the son and heir of the 11th Earl of Southesk and Princess Mazud, second daughter of the 1st Duke of Fife. He lives at Elsick House, Stonehaven, Kincardineshire.

The clan motto is *Deus juvat* — "God assists". The badge is a lion rampant, holding a dagger in its paw.

TARTAN Since the clan MacDuff was not prominent in the later years of Scottish history, this tartan is similar to the royal Stewart without the white and yellow lines. There is a modern hunting tartan. Septs include Fyfe, Hume, Spence and Wemyss.

The MacEwens are an ancient clan, probably descended from the Scots of Dalriada, who have left few records behind them and who were dispossessed of their lands in the 15th century. They then became scattered all over Scotland, which is perhaps why there are about a dozen different ways of spelling the name.

Ewen of Otter, taking his name from a place on the shores of Loch Fyne in Argyllshire, was the first chief, mentioned around 1200, who gave his name to the clan. His castle was on a rocky point below the church of Kilfinnan. Together with the Lamonts, the MacLachlans and the MacNeills, the MacEwens eventually dominated the greater part of Cowal.

In 1431 Swene MacEwen, the 9th and last of the Otter chiefs, granted his lands to the Campbells. After his death, the King confirmed that they belonged to the Earl of Argyll and the MacEwens became a dispossessed clan. At the end of the 16th century, they were described as broken Highland men and trespassers, living like outlaws.

MacEwens are found in Perthshire, Lochaber and as far south as Galloway, though some became hereditary bards of the Campbells. The only landed branch is the MacEwens of Bardrochat, Ayrshire, and Marchmont, Berwickshire. The chief of the clan is not known.

The motto of the Bardrochat MacEwens is *Reviresco* — "I grow green". Their badge is the trunk of an oak tree with branches sprouting from it.

TARTAN Since they were a broken clan by the 16th century, absorbed by the Campbells, the MacEwen tartan is very similar to that of Campbell of Loudoun.

The MacFarlanes are one of the few clans to have descended from the ancient Celtic Earldoms. Their territories commanded the all-important route to the Western Highlands, yet they ended up a broken clan, chiefless and stripped of all their possessions. The clan's ancestor was Gilchrist, whose powerful brother, the Earl of Lennox, gave him lands at Arrochar, on Loch Long. Parlan (Bartholomew in English), the 7th chief, gave the clan its name. The lands of "wild MacFarlane's plaided clan" stretched between Loch Lomond and Loch Long and north to Loch Sloy, a small loch at the foot of Ben Vorlich, the mountain whose name became their war cry.

The MacFarlanes were warlike in a part of Scotland where there were plenty of other clans ready to do battle. They would sally forth in raiding parties from their island fastness of Inveruglas on Loch Lomond by the light of the moon, which became known as "MacFarlane's lantern". Their connection with the Lennoxes also led them into battles in the 15th and 16th centuries, when every second MacFarlane chief died in the field.

When the Earl of Lennox was beheaded in the 15th century the MacFarlanes became the senior members of this great Celtic house and claimed the title. However, it went instead to Stewart of Darnley, who had married Lennox's daughter. Later, however, they sided with the Earl of Lennox after his son, Lord Darnley, Mary Queen of Scots' husband, was murdered and helped defeat her at the battle of Langside.

The MacFarlanes were as turbulent as their neighbours, the MacGregors, and like them, they were proscribed and stripped of their name, after a feud with the Colquhouns of Luss. Some members of the clan emigrated to Ireland, while others were convicted of theft and robbery and despatched to different parts of Scotland where they lived under assumed names. Many settled in Aberdeen and Banffshire under the name Allan or Macallan after the name of the chief's younger son, Allan.

The 20th chief, Walter, a noted antiquarian, died in 1767 and his seat at Arrochar was sold. The last MacFarlane of Macfarlane is thought to have emigrated to America.

The clan motto is "This I'll defend" and its badge a half-naked man holding a sheaf of arrows in one hand and a crown in the other.

TARTAN This MacFarlane tartan is a very complex and the experts doubt that the clan could have retained it after they were broken and dispossessed. There is also a hunting version and another simple black and white design.

An even older form of this surname is MacDuffie. The original home of the clan was the island of Colonsay, off western Argyllshire, which the clan owned until the middle of the 17th century.

MacDuffie of Colonsay was the hereditary keeper of the records of the Lords of the Isles. On the island of Iona there is a tombstone commemorating Malcolm MacDuffie, who married the sister of John MacIan of Ardnamurchan, one of the most powerful of the clan Donald 15th-century chieftains. Another MacDuffie was the prior of Oronsay, the neighbouring island to Colonsay.

In 1615, Malcolm MacFie escaped from Edinburgh Castle and joined Sir James MacDonald of Islay to become one of the leaders in his rebellion against the crown. Later he and some of his followers were were murdered by Coll Kitto MacDonald. From that time on Colonsay was lost to the MacFies, becoming first the property of the MacDonalds, and then of the MacNeils, who retained it until the beginning of this century.

The MacFies became another broken and dispossessed clan. Some followed the MacDonalds of Islay, while others settled in Cameron lands under Lochiel. Ewan McPhee remained rebellious; he became famous as the last of the Scottish "outlaws" in the mid-19th century. He lived with his family on an island in Loch Quoich, defending it with arms against all comers and recognizing no laws.

The MacFies of Langhouse, Renfrewshire, are the most prominent branch of this clan, while the MacFies of Dreghorn are a cadet line.

The motto of the Dreghorn MacFies is *Pro Rege* — "For the King". Their badge is a lion rampant.

TARTAN The MacPhee or MacDuffie tartan appears to be of fairly modern origin, and is a variation of the red MacDonald.

The original homelands of the clan MacGillivrary, one of the oldest branches of the clan Chattan confederacy, were in Morvern, Mull and Lochaber. In the 12th century they were said to be one of the most important clans in Dalriada but by the 18th century many had emigrated across the Atlantic, particularly to Canada, where some made fortunes in the fur trade. When the last chief, John Lachlan MacGillivray of Dunmaglass, Strathnairn, died in 1852, he left all his lands and farms to his tenants.

Founder of the clan is said to have been Gillivray, who in 1268 put himself under the protection of the 5th chief of the Mackintoshes, the leaders of clan Chattan. By that time the clan was already being dispersed, and by 1500 a body of MacGillivrays had settled further north, in Dunmaglass, east Inverness-shire. Here they were more successful and built up quite large landholdings. The attractive churchyard of Dunlichty, near Daviot in Inverness-shire, which was the chiefs' burial place, still has many of their tombstones.

But the Jacobite risings of 1715 and 1745, in which the MacGillivray clan took a prominent part, led to their eventual downfall. In 1715, the laird and his brother were captain and lieutenant in the clan Chattan regiment. The most famous fighting MacGillivray was Alexander, who commanded clan Chattan during the '45 rising. At Culloden, their fierce attack almost decimated the left wing of the Hanoverian army, but the chief himself was killed near the Well of the Dead, which bears his name.

After that the emigrations of the clan began. William MacGillivray became head of the North West Company in Canada, and a member of the legislative council for Lower Canada. He was instrumental in thwarting the Earl of Selkirk's bold plan to settle the destitute Highlanders and Irish Gaels in the Red River settlement. The last chief, John Lachlan MacGillivray, succeeded in 1783 at the time of the clearances, which may be why he felt compelled to leave all his estate to his tenants on his death. The last of that line went to India and was last heard of in New Guinea.

The clan motto is "Dunmaglass", the name of the chief's seat, and its badge a stag's head.

TARTAN The MacGillivray tartan is characteristic of the clan Chattan, incorporating the light blue lines very often found in the tartans of clans from the Morvern and nearby areas.

Septs include Gilroy, MacIlroy, Milroy and Roy.

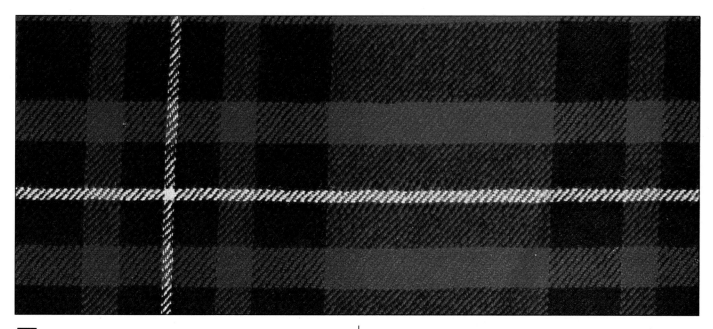

The very fact that the MacGregors still have a chief is a tribute to their amazing staying power and pugnacity. Outlawed with a high price on their heads, forbidden to hold meetings of more than four members of the clan, hounded by the government and banned for more than a century from even using the name MacGregor, they still managed to survive. The 23rd chief is Colonel Sir Gregor MacGregor of MacGregor, who has had a distinguished military career and who lives at Bannatyne, Newtyle, Angus.

That bold buccaneer, Rob Roy MacGregor, epitomizes the fiery, unquenchable spirit of his clansmen, who claim descent from the royal Celtic line of King Alpin. Their motto is their boast — *S rioghal mo dhream*, Gaelic for "Royal is my race". Their clan lands were on the borders of Perthshire and Argyllshire, and included Glenorchy, Glenstrae, Glenlyon and Glengyle. Unfortunately, they held their territories by right of occupation, not by legal deeds. As their neighbours, the Campbells, became more powerful they managed to get crown charters to lands which had been in MacGregor possession for many years.

This is how the MacGregors acquired their warlike reputation, when they fought to keep their inheritance by the sword. Originally called MacGregor of Glenorchy after their estates, the chief of that name was captured by the English in 1296 and his property passed to a Campbell, after which Gregor MacGregor began the long war to retrieve the clan's rights.The chiefship passed to the Macgregors of Glenstrae but even they were tenants of the Campbells, who constantly tried to destroy the Macgregors, at one time setting up a rival line of chiefs and later killing off three generations of the chiefship line.

Neighbouring chiefs also were encouraged to pursue the MacGregors who, by now, lived by raiding and killing. King James VI saw them as the "wicked and unhappie race of the clan Gregour" and as they continued to flout his authority, he determined to deal with them once and for all. His opportunity came in 1603 when, against this background of constant strife with the Campbells and the crown, the MacGregors took on the Colquhouns, holders of the royal commission. At the Battle of Glenfruin in 1603 the MacGregors massacred the Colquhouns and carried off their cattle and other livestock.

The King immediately outlawed them, and any who were captured were, like Alasdair the chief, immediately executed. On the day he left Edinburgh to mount the English throne as James I of England he passed an act to proscribe the clan and abolish their name. A price of £1,000 was put on the heads of the clan leaders, and 100 merks on those of lesser clansmen. Later, further measures were introduced, banning them from carrying arms, except for "ane pointless knife to cut their meat", and from more than four meeting together, even under different names.

In 1606 it was decreed that even the clan's unborn children could not use the name MacGregor, which was when various surnames like Dougall, Drummond, Gordon, Graham, Grant, Murray and Ramsay were adopted. Even 40 years later acts were still being passed to make the name MacGregor unlawful, to ban ministers from baptising the male children and to grant any who murdered them legal impunity.

Although the clan rallied to the Royalist cause, supporting the Marquis of Montrose against the government's supporters, the Campbells, Charles I was no kinder to them. However, Charles II restored their name, though not their lands, in 1663, because of their affection and loyalty. Yet only 30 years later, because of their support for the Jacobites, the ban was reimposed, not to be finally lifted until 1775.

Even Rob Roy MacGregor, whose wife, Mary, evidently composed the pipe tune "Rob Roy's Lament", was able to come out of hiding. He was imprisoned in Newgate prison and was just about to be deported to Barbados when his pardon came through. He died peacefully in 1734 at his home in Balquidder, Perthshire, where he is buried in the little local churchyard, but his rebellious ways were inherited by some of his five sons. One was executed, one fled to France and another was attainted for fighting in the '45, though he too was later pardoned.

TARTAN Rob Roy has a tartan all to himself, though why this should be is something of a mystery. This simple red and black check is the older of the two MacGregor tartans; a later one with a red background and green and black checks is thought to be the dress tartan.

Because of the banning of their name, there are dozens of different sept names of this clan.

·MACINTYRE·

·MACKAY·

The origin of this clan name is from the Gaelic *Mac-an-t-saoir*, which means "son of the carpenter". Of ancient origin, it has a close connection with the clan Donald. Many of the clan emigrated in the 18th and 19th centuries, some to Canada, others to the United States of America. By 1792 the chief had died in America, but his descendants were said to be living in Fulton, New York, and thus in 1921 the chief was an American businessman.

The clan, which later became widespread throughout Scotland, was originally associated with Lorn, in north Argyllshire, where the Macintyres of Glencoe became hereditary foresters to the Stewarts of Lorn. They were the principal branch of the clan until, in 1806, they gave up their estate and emigrated to America.

By tradition the Macintyres sailed from the Hebrides to Lorn in a galley with a white cow around 1360 and established themselves in Glen Noe, near Bonawe, Argyllshire. These lands were held on tenure from the Campbells of Glenorchy, for an annual summer payment of a snowball and a white fatted calf. In the Scottish mountains a snowball was not quite so difficult to find at the height of summer as it sounds, since there was always snow lying in the deep gullies at the back of Cruachan. Rather stupidly, the Macintyres changed this arrangement at the beginning of the 18th century, offering to pay money instead of a snowball, which meant that their rent could be continually increased to the point where they could not meet it. In 1783, one of the three sons of James Macintyre of Glen Noe emigrated to Canada, and by 1808 these estates had been sold.

The Macintyres were men of many parts, some becoming hereditary pipers, both to the MacDonald of Clanranald and to the Menzies chiefs. Another branch was renowned for their weaving of hose and garters. One of the most famous Gaelic poets was Duncan Macintyre, who was born in Glenorchy in 1724. He was put in prison for writing a poem against the banning of the Highland dress and died in 1812. A memorial was erected to him in Greyfriars Churchyard, Edinburgh.

The clan motto is *Per ardua* — "Through difficulties". The badge is a hand holding a dirk on which is impaled a snowball.

TARTAN There are three Macintyre tartans, two of which are called Macintyre and Glenorchy. The experts describe the double-named tartan as a district one, pointing out that no Macintyre arms were ever registered at the Lyon court. It is this third tartan, the Macintyre hunting, which is more generally accepted.

The Mackays were the clan most remote in distance from the Scottish government, holding lands from Cape Wrath in the northwest to the Caithness border. Yet their Gaelic was closer to that of southern Ireland than to the Scottish version, and the clan patronymic, *Aodh*, goes back to early Irish folktales.

They are first recorded as opposing Donald of the Isles, when the chief of the clan Mackay, Angus Dhu Mackay, had 4,000 men to defend his territories. Until the 17th century all the Mackay chiefs married into the Gaelic aristocracy of Scotland, including the Lord of the Isles' family.

The MacKays also had to battle against the powerful Earldom of Sutherland, which had passed into Gordon possession after the Battle of Flodden. Indeed, the 10 or more clan battles which the Mackays fought only resulted in the loss of their manpower, so much so that by the 1745 uprising they could only raise 800 clansmen.

They won honour and glory, not so much in the clan skirmishes of Scotland, as on the battlegrounds of Europe. By 1626 Donald, chief of the Mackays, had raised 3,000 clansmen to fight in the European wars. At the same time as the Mackays were fighting in support of Charles I's sister, Elizabeth of Bohemia, under the Danish and Swedish Kings, they also became Barons of Nova Scotia.

General Aeneas Mackay decided to make his home in Holland, where his great-grandson was made Baron Mackay of Ophemert. The military tradition was carried on when Hugh Mackay, serving with the Scots Brigade in Holland, joined William of Orange and commanded the forces against Bonnie Dundee at Killiecrankie. Both Dundee and Mackay were killed.

However, by 1875 the direct line of Mackay chiefs had died out. The title then passed to the Dutch branch, who had been ennobled in the 17th century. The present chief of the clan is Hugh, 14th Lord Reay, Baron Mackay van Ophemert, whose father became a naturalized British subject in 1938.

The clan motto is *Manu forti* — "With a strong hand" — and the badge is a hand holding a dagger.

TARTAN There are two Mackay tartans, closely resembling the tartan of their near neighbours in the North, the Gunns, with the alteration of the centre line in black instead of red.

There are many septs of this clan, including Allan, Bain, Kay, MacBain, MacCaw, MacGee, Mackie, MacQuoid, MacVain, Morgan, Neilson, Paul and Reay.

The fate of the clan MacKenzie was famously foretold by the Brahan Seer (Brahan, near Dingwall, was where their castle stood until it was demolished in the mid-20th century). Having risen from obscurity to hold lands which stretched right across Scotland, and to become one of the four most important Highland chiefs in 1726 (the others were the Dukes of Argyll, Atholl and Gordon), Lord Seaforth's line ended in the 19th century when all four of his sons died before him.

Legend has it that the clan Kenneth or MacKenzie was founded by an Irish Fitzgerald who brought troops to fight for the Scottish King against the Norsemen at the Battle of Largs and was rewarded with lands in Kintail, Wester Ross. More likely, they are descended from Gilleon Og, a younger son of the Earl of Ross. The first mention of the *Clann Choinnich* is in 1362, when Murdo, son of Kenneth of Kintail, was given a charter to his lands by the King. Some two centuries later the clan had territories which stretched from the Outer Hebrides right across Scotland to the Black Isle.

Alasdair MacKenzie, the 7th chief, who died in 1488, was the most prominent supporter of the crown against the all-powerful Lord of the Isles and got his reward in forfeited MacDonald lands. Originally in Kintail around Loch Duich with Eilean Donan Castle as their base, they spread throughout Ross-shire, and into Lewis on the Outer Hebrides. They moved their seat to Kinellan, near Strathpeffer, before building Brahan Castle.

Alasdair's son, Kenneth, died in 1492 and his stone effigy can still be seen at Beauly Priory, where he was buried. Iain, his son, fought at both Flodden and Pinkie, but survived and lived until the mid-16th century. The MacKenzies continued their rise to power by joining with the forces of Mary, Queen of Scots, and James VI against their Gaelic neighbours. In 1609, the chief was made Lord MacKenzie of Kintail, while in 1623 his eldest son became the Earl of Seaforth. The 2nd earl was Charles II's Secretary of State for Scotland. Another branch of the MacKenzies became the Earls of Cromartie.

It was the Mackenzies' loyalty to the Stewart Kings which brought about their downfall. Kenneth, the 4th Earl, one of the first Knights of the Thistle, the Scottish order of chivalry, followed James VII into exile at the end of the 17th century, the time when the Brahan Seer first predicted doom for his house. The 5th Earl raised an army of 3,000 men in 1715 for the Jacobite pretender, and had to flee to France, returning in 1719 to be severely wounded at Glenshiel. Several MacKenzies took part in the 1745 rebellion.

Although their influence was now waning, Kenneth, the 6th Earl, was made Viscount Fortrose and Baron Ardelve, an Irish peerage, in 1766, and had the title of Earl of Seaforth restored in 1771. In gratitude the chief raised the 1,000-strong 72nd regiment, the old Seaforth Highlanders. But he died without male heirs in 1784 and his titles became extinct. The chiefship and estates passed to his cousin, Colonel Thomas MacKenzie, the great-grandson of the 3rd Earl. Shortly afterwards, he was killed commanding the Bombay army in India at the battle of Gheriah. His younger brother, Francis, succeeded him, only to have all his sons die before him and to have to dispose of much of the MacKenzie land before he himself, the last male descendant of the MacKenzies of Kintail, died in 1815.

His daughter, Mary, was given the MacKenzie arms as Lady Hood-MacKenzie, and from her descend the Stewart-MacKenzies of Seaforth. Her son sold up all the estate except for Brahan and a small part of the clan heartland. Her grandson was made Lord Seaforth of Brahan in 1921, but he, too, died without male heirs, and Brahan Castle was demolished just after World War II. The Earl of Cromartie, who renounced his family name of Blunt to inherit the title through the female line, is now chief of the clan MacKenzie. He lives at Castle Leod, Strathpeffer, Ross-shire.

The MacKenzie clan lands of Kintail, a magnificent 14,000 acres of Highland scenery which include the towering mountains known as the Five Sisters of Kintail, are now in good hands. They were acquired by the National Trust for Scotland in 1944, and mountaineers, campers and walkers now enjoy the land of the MacKenzies. The Trust also looks after another MacKenzie inheritance, the sub-tropical, exotic gardens created out of a barren peninsula at Inverewe in a lattitude more northerly than Moscow, begun by Osgood MacKenzie in 1862 and presented to the Trust in 1952 by his daughter, Mrs. Mairi Sawyer.

Septs of the clan include Charles, Clunies, Cromarty, Ivory, Kenneth, MacIver, MacKenna, MacMurchie, MacQuennie, MacVanish, MacWhinnie and Smart.

The clan motto is *Cuidich 'n righ* — "Help the King". The badge is a stag's head.

TARTAN The regimental tartan of the Seaforth Highlanders, raised by the chief in 1778, green with black checks, is the same as the Athol Murray, except for the replacement of the outer red stripes with white. It is thought that the MacKenzie tartan worn before 1778 was probably a red one.

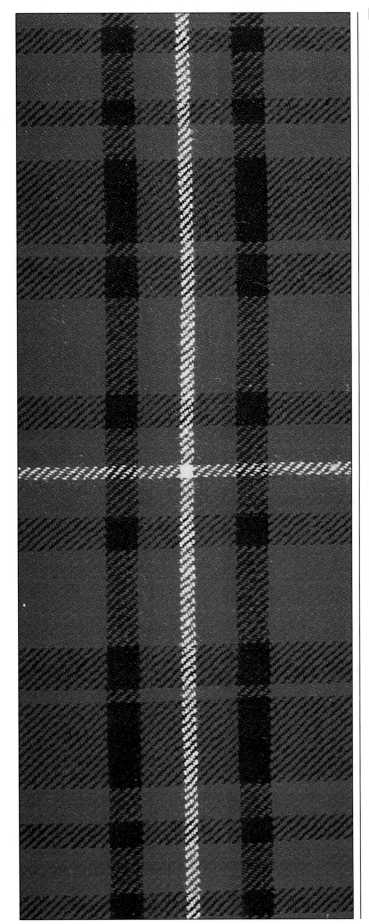

The MacKinnon clan, or clan Fingon after its founder, began with a Prince of the royal house of Kenneth MacAlpin, and therefore was part of the blue-blooded Siol Alpine confederation of clans. Never a powerful clan, though the chiefs had various hereditary posts under the MacDonalds of the Isles, it is a prime example of a clan almost destroyed by its Jacobite sympathies and of a chiefship saved by emigrant clansmen.

The ancient clan lands were in the western isles of Mull, Tiree, Scalpa and Arran, but their principal designation was Strathordell on Skye, lands they received after losing their Mull territories to the Macleans. They were closely involved in the religious life of Iona, where Iain MacKinnon, who died in 1500, was the last abbot. His father erected a Celtic cross, which can still be seen there, as can the stone effigy of the last abbot.

More prosaically, the MacKinnons were the hereditary inspectors of weights and measures for the Lords of the Isles, as well, evidently, as having to settle gambling disputes for them. They had a great castle at Dunakin, guarding the narrows at Kyleakin between Skye and the mainland. After the Lord of the Isles lost his title and power, the MacKinnons threw in their lot with the Macleans of Duart and sided with the MacDonalds of Skye in their feuds with the MacLeods.

But it was their unswerving loyalty to the Stewarts which brought about their eventual downfall. Sir Lachlan Mackinnon, the 28th chief, was knighted by Chales II on the field at Worcester in 1651 before Cromwell destroyed the Scottish army. They were out for the Stewarts in both 1715 and 1745, with a following of over 200 men from the isles. The chief helped Bonnie Prince Charlie escape after Culloden, hiding him in a cave at Strathordell. But later the aged chief was himself captured and imprisoned for a year in Tilbury Fort. Released because of his age, he was still defiant. When the English Attorney General reminded him of the Hanoverian King's clemency towards him, the MacKinnon retorted: "Had I the King in my power, as I am in his, I would return him the compliment by sending him back to his own country".

His son, Charles, found the estates so heavily in debt that in 1791 he had to sell Strathordell, which had been in MacKinnon hands for nearly five centuries. When his son, John, succeeded him, nothing was left but the title of chief, and he died in poverty in 1808. The chiefship passed to Donald, the second son of the 28th chief, who had been knighted on the battlefield of Worcester and later emigrated to Antigua in the West Indies where he made his fortune. His descendant, Alasdair MacKinnon of MacKinnon, lives at Orchard Cottage, Nailsbourne, near Taunton, Somerset.

The clan motto is *Audentes fortuna juvat* — "Fortune favours the brave". The badge is a boar's head with a deer bone in its mouth.

TARTAN There are two MacKinnon tartans, the more modern of which is a hunting tartan. Septs include Love, MacKinven, MacMorran and Sherry.

The fact that Lt. Cdr. Lachlan Mackintosh of Mackintosh still lives today at Moy Hall, Moy, Inverness-shire, seat of the clan for over 600 years, is a tribute to the astuteness of his predecessors, those long-time natural leaders of the clan Chattan, the powerful confederation of Highland clans. They steered the Mackintoshes through the hazards of choosing the right side to follow, managing also to ward off the attacks of more powerful clans, though they earned the rather dubious distinction of being defeated in the last clan battle fought with the MacDonells and MacKenzies at Mulroy in 1688. Later chiefs took part in the American War of Independence and lived in Canada and the West Indies.

The name comes from the Gaelic *Mac-an-Toisich*, Gaelic for "son of the chief", who is traditionally said to have been a thane of the royal house of MacDuff. In 1163, Shaw, second son of the Earl of Fife, who is thought to be the first chief, was given lands in Moray and made Keeper of Inverness Castle by King Malcolm IV. Marriage with the heiress of clan Chattan brought lands in the west. Three centuries later the Mackintoshes had estates which stretched from Lochaber in the west to Petty on the shores of the Moray Firth, as well as the fertile valleys of the Nairn, Findhorn and the Spey.

The 6th Chief's support for Robert the Bruce brought them the barony of Moy. The 10th chief, equally wisely, fought on the side of the crown in the 15th century instead of with his overlord, the Lord of the Isles, whose empire was beginning to crumble. This brought the clan the Lochaber lands and other properties in the west.

Other chiefs were less fortunate. The 12th was kidnapped and imprisoned by the King in various Lowland castles, including Edinburgh and Stirling, from 1497 to 1513. The 15th crossed swords with the powerful Gordons and was murdered in the kitchens of the Gordons of Huntly in the mid-16th century.

A more unusual attempt to tame the Mackintoshes was made by James VI, who ordered Sir Lachlan Mackintosh, the 17th chief, to be educated at Oxford or Cambridge so that he might become more anglicized. Despite this, the clan supported the Stewart Kings and fought off, in the law courts this time, an attempt by the MacPhersons to take over the leadership of the clan Chattan in the 17th century. Led gallantly by their chief, Lachlan, the clan took part in the first Jacobite rising of 1715, though during the second rising in 1745 the 22nd chief was a captain in the Black Watch and remained loyal to the Hanoverian army.

A remarkable woman then emerged to lead the clan into battle for Bonnie Prince Charlie. She was his young wife, Anne, the daughter of Farquharson of Invercauld, who raised 400 clansmen and earned the nickname "Colonel Anne" because of her bold military strategy. She put the chief of the clan Mac-Gillvray at the head of clan Chattan and won the famous encounter known as the "Rout of Moy" when they defeated the much larger force led by Lord Loudon.

The 23rd chief also fought for the Hanoverian King, this time across the Atlantic at the Battle of Brooklyn in 1776. The chief died without an heir, and the chiefship passed to a Mackintosh who had become a Jamaican merchant, and from him to a shipowner on the Canadian lakes, from whom the present chief is descended.

When the 28th chief died in 1938 he settled the Mackintosh title and Moy Hall on his junior cousin, Lachlan Donald, while the 32nd chiefship of clan Chattan went to the other Mackintosh heir at law. The present chief of the clan Chattan, Malcolm Kenneth Mackintosh, lives in Gwelo, Zimbabwe.

The clan motto is the same as that of the clan Chattan, "Touch not the cat without a glove", as is their badge of a wild cat.

There are many septs including Adamson, Cash, Clark, Crerar, Dallas, Easson, Eggo, Elder, Hardy, Mactavish, MacThomas, Tawse and Tosh.

TARTAN The red Mackintosh tartan (see page 21), with its black and green checks is one of the very few ancient tartans which is completely authentic. There are three other tartans, one of which is for the chief's use and is described as having a "very showy pattern". Another version of the clan tartan includes a white stripe, but is not considered to be so geniune as the first. This green hunting Mackintosh is a modern design.

The clan MacLachlan, one of the most ancient Scottish clans, may also be part of the oldest family in Europe, the descendants of the 5th-century Irish royal family, the O'Neills. Aedh, a grandson of the 11th-century Irish King, Flaithbertach, is said to have married a Scottish Princess, the heiress to the Kingdom of Cowal.

Madam MacLachlan of MacLachlan, the 24th chief, is the direct decendant of a line that can be traced back through records for at least seven centuries. The clan heartland of Strathlachlan, near Loch Fyne Argyll, where the chief still lives in Castle Lachlan, is believed to have belonged to the MacLachlans since the 11th century.

The MacLachlans intermarried with the Kings of Kerry and the Lords of the Isles, as well as with their Cowal neighbours, the Lamonts and the MacEwen. The clan supported Robert the Bruce, even though it was the King he displaced, John Balliol, who gave Gileskil (or Gillespie) MacLachlan the first charter to his Argyllshire lands. The MacLachlans were also staunch supporters of the Celtic church, possibly because St. Columba had himself been of the O'Neill royal line.

In 1680 Lachlan MacLachlan had his lands of Strathlachlan made into a barony, and although not far from the Campbell courts of Inveraray, he still kept his independent power to try offenders. The MacLachlan of Coruanan, Lochaber, the main cadet branch of the clan, were hereditary standard bearers to the Camerons of Lochiel.

The MacLachlans were loyal to the Stewarts. The 17th chief raised his clan for Bonnie Prince Charlie and became his A.D.C., but as he rode at the head of his troops into battle at Culloden he was killed by a cannonball. Castle Lachlan was bombarded and reduced to ruins, though the 18th chief, through the intercession of the Duke of Argyll, got his lands back and a new Castle Lachlan was built in the 19th century.

When John MacLachlan, the 23rd chief, died in 1942, his daughter Marjorie, became the first female to succeed to the chiefship.

The clan motto is *Fortis et Fidus* — "Brave and trusty". The badge is a three-towered castle perched on top of a coronet.

TARTAN There are three MacLachlan tartans. The chief wears a brilliant combination of yellow and black. The other two are of ancient design, with the clan generally wearing this red and dark blue design. Septs include Eunson, Ewing, Gilchrist, Lachie and MacKeon.

The *Clann Labhran* has confused origins. It may be called after Laurin (or Lawrence), the hereditary Celtic abbot of Achtus, Balquidder, Perthshire, which became the clan seat. Its rallying cry is *Creag an Tuire* "the boar's rock", which stands near Achtow in Balquhidder. In medieval times, the clan seems to have been important, as kinsmen of the powerful Celtic Earls of Strathearn. However, once the Earldom of Strathearn had been seized by the crown in 1379, the MacLarens fell with it, becoming mere tenants, though they still had their own chief. By then, they were followers of the Stewart Lords of Lorn. One of the sons fell in love with the daughter of MacLaurin of Ardveche and their son, Dugald, legitimized on their marriage, founded the Stewarts of Appin.

As early as the 1500s MacLarens began to emigrate, becoming mercenaries in Europe and serving with the French and Italian armies. This accelerated after they were twice overrun by the lawless MacGregor clan in the 1500s, when families were slaughtered and their lands seized. Many enlisted in the Swedish army during the Thirty Years War.

Yet the clan was still able to raise men for the Jacobite risings, both in 1715 and 1745. After Culloden, their leader, Donald of Invernenty, was captured but managed to make a dramatic escape at the Devil's Beef Tub, the great hollow in the hills near Moffat, while being taken to Carlisle prison. Sir Walter Scott describes this incident in his novel *Redgauntlet*.

The MacLarens of Invernentie were the cause of Sir Walter Scott's first visit to the Highlands, which he was to write about afterwards in *Rob Roy*. As a young lawyer, he went to Balquhidder with a troop of soldiers in 1790 to serve an eviction order on a MacLaren tenant. He found the house was empty because the family had already emigrated to Canada. The head of Invernenty, still lives in Canada and established his status as a cadet branch of the MacLarens in 1962.

The MacLarens of Auchleskine are recognized as the main branch of the Perthshire clan, and in 1957 Donald MacLaren became the clan chief. His son, Donald, now the MacLaren of MacLaren, is in the British foreign service.

The MacLaurins of Tiree, a separate island race, had a chief in the 18th century, Lord Dreghorn, but that line has died out.

The clan badge is a crowned lion's head.

TARTAN The MacLaren tartan is very similar to that of the Fergusons, their Perthshire neighbours, the only difference being a yellow line where the Ferguson has a white one. Septs include Faed, Law, Lowe, MazcFeat, MacGrory, Peterkin and Rorison.

The Macleans of Duart are recognized as the head of the clan Maclean, a great sea-faring tribe which spread far and wide throughout the Highlands and Islands of Scotland after it was founded by Gillean of the Battleaxe, who fought at the 13th-century Battle of Largs against the Norsemen. Most clan Maclean branches still incorporate a battle-axe in their badges in his memory.

Dramatic Duart Castle, on its rocky promontory overlooking the Sound of Mull, built in the 14th century, was given to Lachlan Maclean after he married Mary MacDonald, daughter of the Lord of the Isles, along with other lands in Mull. Today the 27th clan chief, Lord Maclean, a life peer, Lord Chamberlain to Her Majesty's Household, and, from 1959 to 1975, Chief Scout of the Commonwealth, still lives there, though only because his grandfather, Sir Fitzroy Maclean, who lived to be 101 years old, bought back and restored the ancient ruins in 1912.

The Macleans of Duart had held the earlier office of Chamberlain to the Lord of the Isles, a title which was confirmed by the crown in 1495 even after the Lordship was abolished. The clan Maclean's extensive lands included the islands of Mull, Tiree, Coll and Islay, as well as mainland Morvern and Lochaber. As the clan expanded, it split into a number of different branches, including the Macleans of Coll and the Macleans of Ardgour.

The most senior of these, were the Maclaines of Lochbuie on Mull, descended from Hector, the brother of Lachlan of Duart (despite the variation in spelling) and often disputed their right to the chiefship with the Macleans of Duart, arguing that Hector was the elder brother. However, Lachlan of Duart had not been given the nickname of "the wily one" for nothing, and his successors proved that they, too, knew their way around the political scene. Lachlan's son, Hector, managed to wangle a safe passage through England from Henry IV so that he could visit the imprisoned Scottish King James I. Another Lachlan chief was a special agent for Queen Elizabeth I of England in the 16th century and tried to bargain with her, threatening to use Highland mercenaries to help the Irish rebels. He was killed in 1598 and his sons massacred the people of Islay in revenge.

Perhaps the most notorious Maclean chief was the one who put his wife, a sister of the Earl of Argyll, on a tidal rock in the Sound of Mull, known to this day as the Lady Rock. Expecting her to drown, he announced her death to the Campbells, prematurely as it turned out. Passing fishermen had rescued her, and in 1523 her brother, Campbell of Cawdor, avenged her by stabbing her cruel husband to death in Edinburgh.

At the height of the MacLachlans' power in the 17th century Sir Lachlan was made a Baronet of Nova Scotia in 1633 but had to borrow money from Argyll for the family debts. Only two years after his death, his son, Sir Hector, died fighting for Charles II on the battlefield at Inverkeithing. Seven brothers of the clan each gave their lives to protect the chief, crying as they fell "Another for Hector", now the clan's war cry.

By the end of the 17th century the Argylls had called in their debts and had possession of Duart estate, while the chief went into exile. Sir Hector, the 5th Baronet, returned in 1745 to raise the clan, only to be captured and imprisoned in London. When he died in exile in Italy the direct line became extinct.

The chiefship went to Alan Maclean of Brolas, under the terms of a charter of 1466. The chief of the Macleans of Coll emigrated to South Africa in 1848, leaving the Georgian house where he had entertained Dr. Johnson and James Boswell on their Highland tour to become derelict, although the tower castle by the shore has recently been restored by a Maclean descendant. Donald, the 20th chief of the Maclaine of Lochbuie, whose estates were burdened with debts, went to Java in 1816 and made a fortune which enabled him to clear them, but by his grandson's time an Englishman had impounded the ancient castle.

The clan motto is "Virtue mine honour" and the badge a tower with battlements.

TARTAN This green and black hunting Maclean tartan with white stripes may date back to the 16th century, though there is no evidence to prove this. The Maclean dress tartan is the same design as the Royal Stewart, though the pattern is reversed. The Maclaines of Lochbuie also have two tartans, but in their case the hunting is the modern one, while the other is thought to date from the 18th century. The Macleans have many septs.

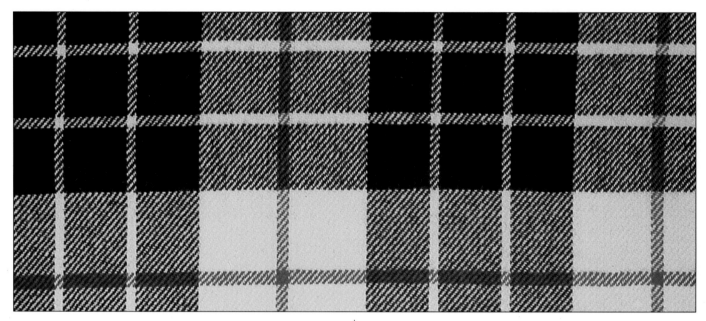

Dunvegan Castle, on Skye, "the hearth of the race", has been occupied by the MacLeod chiefs for more than seven centuries and is the oldest inhabited castle in Scotland. Standing almost sea-girt on a rock, it contains such clan treasures as the "fairy flag" with its threefold magical powers; if waved on the battlefield it increases the numbers of Macleods; over a marriage bed it promises fertility; over the loch it brings the herring shoals. According to tradition it has been waved twice with the promised results, but if the third wave is used the flag bearer will disappear from the earth.

The reality is that the cream-coloured silk flag, embroidered in gold, is more than 1,000 years old and is of eastern Mediterranean origin. This would fit in with the origins of the clan itself, the name coming from Leod, son of Olaf, King of Man and the North Isles, a member of the royal Norse line of Godred, King of Dublin and Man. One of the Norse Kings was said to have brought back a sacred relic from Constantinople, and some historians believe that may be the fairy flag.

Leod himself, by his 13th-century marriage to the heiress of Macarailt of Dunvegan, had two sons, Tormod (or Norman in English) and Torquil, and from them descend the two main lines of the clan. The *Siol Tormod* were the Macleods of Macleod and Harris while the *Siol Torquil* were the Macleods of Lewis. From Tormod, the elder son, who inherited Dunvegan, come the Macleods of Glenelg, Harris, and Dunvegan, while Torquil's descendants are the Macleods of Lewis, Waternish and Assynt.

The line of the Macleods of Lewis did not last beyond the 16th century and the 11th chief. Roderick, the 10th chief, passed over his elder son in favour of the younger brother, Torquil, who was murdered by his disinherited brother. The chiefship then passed to the Earls of Cromartie (who still bear the title Baron Macleod, as well as being chiefs of the clan MacKenzie).

The 5th chief had given one of his younger sons his lands of Assynt, in Sutherland, where Macleods still live today. The one-time chief of this line, the debt-ridden Neil of Assynt, is still reviled for selling the hunted Marquis of Montrose to the Roundheads for 400 bolls of meal, with the result that the Marquis was executed on the Edinburgh scaffold. After this "deed of deathless shame" the line itself withered and died.

The senior branch of the Macleods of Lewis then became the Macleods of Raasay, the island to the east of Skye, but by 1846 Raasay had been sold and the chief had emigrated to Australia, where his descendants now live.

Tormod's line were survivors, helped by the fine calibre of some of their chiefs. The 8th chief, the cultured Alasdair the Crottach (Hump-backed), added the fairy tower to Dunvegan and in 1547 was buried in a splendid tomb at St. Clement's Church, which he had rebuilt, at Rodel, on Harris. He is also said to have been the first to encourage playing the bagpipes.

This had come into full artistic flowering by the time of the great Rory Mor, the 15th chief, knighted by James VI in 1603, who also added a new extension to Dunvegan Castle. He was revered by the clan and the famous *piobaireachd* "Rory Mor's Lament" was composed by Patrick MacCrimmon on his death in 1626. Alasdair Crottach's sword and Rory Mor's horn can still be seen at Dunvegan.

The Macleods were supporters of Charles I; 700 clansmen were slaughtered at the battle of Worcester in 1651. This may have been the reason why they showed little enthusiasm for the later Jacobite cause.

Many Macleods emigrated, particularly after the famine in Skye in the 1840s. One of the most famous emigrés was the Assynt minister, Norman Macleod, who took his congregation with him in 1817 to found a new community at Pictou, in Nova Scotia. Hearing his son extol life in the Antipodes, the 71-year-old Macleod once more uprooted his flock, numbering 747 by now, and took them this time to Waipu, in New Zealand.

The race of great chiefs continued even into this century, when in 1935 Dame Flora Macleod of Macleod succeeded her father, the last of the direct male line, as 28th chief. Even when well into her eighties, this redoubtable lady travelled all over the world to meet her overseas kith and kin and to keep the clan in touch. Dame Flora started the clan "Parliament" and made Dunvegan the clan centre again. She was succeeded in 1976 by her younger grandson, John Wolridge Gordon, who changed his name to take over the proud title of Macleod of Macleod, become the 29th chief and carry on the very long line at Dunvegan.

The clan motto is "Hold fast" and the badge is a bull's head between two flags.

TARTAN The Macleods have two tartans, one this highly distinctive design in yellow and black. In a letter written to Sir Walter Scott in 1829 it was described as a "splendid" tartan, though other critics of the time likened it to a horse blanket! The second tartan is a more sober dark green, with blue and black checks and red and yellow stripes.

Septs include Beaton, Grimmond, Harold, MacCaig, Mac-Clure, MacCrimmon, MacWilliam and Norman.

The Macmillans are a clan of uncertain origins but their name is perpetuated as permanently overseas as it is in Scotland. There is, for instance, a town called Macmillan in America and a Macmillan river in British Columbia, while it was an Angus Macmillan who discovered the area of Gippsland in Victoria, Australia.

It may have been ecclesiastical origins that allowed the Macmillans passively to be moved off their lands time and again. In Gaelic a Macmillan is called *Mac-Mhaoilean*, meaning "son of the tonsured one". In the Celtic church the front half of the head was shaved, which probably means that the Macmillans are descended from hereditary abbots.

They appear first at Loch Arkaig, Inverness-shire, but were moved from there in the 12th century by the King and resettled on crown lands at Lawers in Perthshire. Yet again they were driven off these lands in the 14th century, and took themselves West to Knapdale, in mid-Argyllshire, while others went further south into Galloway.

In Knapdale they became more important in the 15th century, and acquired land through marriage to the heiress of the MacNeills, who had Castle Sween. The Macmillan tower was added to the castle and a cross in Kilmory churchyard commemorates the chief.

The Macmillan lands were lost when the Lord of the Isles fell from power and the line of the chiefs of Knap later became extinct. Macmillan of Dunmore, whose estate was on the north side of Loch Tarbert, became the chief. In 1767 Alexander Macmillan of Dunmore settled the estate on his cousin, Duncan Macmillan of Laggalgarve, but he died unmarried.

In 1951 Lieut. General Sir Gordon Macmillan, then G.O.C Scottish Command, was recognized as chief of the clan Macmillan by the Lord Lyon.

The clan motto is *Miseris succurrere disco* — "I learn to succour the distressed". The badge is a hand brandishing a double-handed sword.

TARTAN This Macmillan old tartan is a colourful combination of yellow on a crimson and green background. The modern hunting tartan carries through the same colour scheme but imposes it on the more conventional blue, black and green designs of the darker tartans.

Septs include Baxter, Bell, Blue, Brown and MacNamell.

For a clan descended from hereditary churchmen — the name comes from *Clann-An-Aba*, meaning "children of the Abbot" — the MacNabs have produced a rich crop of buccaneers and brigands.

Canada was where the MacNabs' most notorious leader, Archibald, the 13th chief, attempted to establish a new clan homeland, using his kinsmen virtually as feudal serfs. Having sold off the clan lands and fled Scotland in 1820 to escape his creditors, leaving his wife and eight children behind, he headed for Montreal, where he was received with open arms by several hundred MacNabs already living there. He was given a grant of 80,000 acres of undeveloped land in Ontario and, treating as his vassals the 21 McNab families who had emigrated with him, he tried to recoup the family fortunes. By 1830 he had more than 60 families at his mercy and had fathered an illegitimate son by his housekeeper.

In 1843 his exploitation of his kinsmen was brought into the open and he was convicted in the Canadian courts. When he sued for libel he was awarded a mere $10 damages for the defamation of the MacNab of MacNab's character.

Sir Allan MacNab (1798—1862) became Prime Minister of the Canadas. Another migrant MacNab, Robert, became a leading politician in New Zealand during World War II.

The most outrageously flamboyant of all the MacNab chiefs, Francis, is immortalized for us as *The MacNab* in the famous portrait of him by Raeburn. He fathered children all over the MacNab lands but died in 1816 without leaving a legitimate heir, having squandered the clan's patrimony. This led to the succession of his nephew, the notorious 13th chief, Archibald, who so grievously misled his trusting clansmen in Canada.

James Charles MacNab of MacNab, who lives at Wester Kilmany House, Cupar, Fife, succeeded as 23rd chief in 1970.

The clan motto is *Timor omnis abesto* — "Let fear be far from all" — and the badge is the head of a male savage.

TARTAN Using the same pattern as the Black Watch but in different colours, this most commonly worn of the three MacNab tartans is vividly colourful. The chief's tartan is even more striking, with a greater use of crimson, and the third design also combines red and crimson.

Septs include Abbot, Clelland, Dewar, Gilland, MacLellan and MacNair.

Northern Ireland has been the home of the hereditary chiefs of the Macnaghtens — the spelling the present chief uses — for nearly 200 years. John Dhu Macnaghten, a brother of the Laird of Dundarave, the picturesque clan castle on Loch Fyne, settled in Antrim in about 1580. In 1818 his descendant, Edmund Macnaghten of Bushmills, Antrim, claimed the hereditary chiefship; 400 members of the clan witnessed his claim and it was confirmed by the Lord Lyon. Today Sir Patrick Macnaghten of Macnaghten is the chief and still lives at Bushmills.

Nechtan was the name of the Pictish Kings, commemorated by the famous victory won by the King of the Picts in 685 at Nechtansmere against the invading English. The clan lands were around Loch Awe, Glenara, Glenshira and on Loch Fyne, where their now restored castle of Dundarave bears the 1596 inscription above the door *Behold the End. Be not Wiser than the Highest. I Hope in God.* They were also, in the 13th century, made keepers of the King's island castle of *Fraoch Eilean* (the name is the clan's war cry) on Loch Awe.

By the end of the 14th century, after opposing Robert the Bruce, the Macnaghtens had lost their Loch Awe lands to the Campbells, though later they were recompensed with lands on the island of Lewis, part of the forfeited MacDonald property. Thereafter, and for the next 300 years, Dundarave, the "Castle of the Two Oars", for which Gilbert Macnachten had received a charter in 1473 from the Earl of Argyll, became the clan heartland. The last chief to live there, an Inspector-General of Customs, died in 1773, but the present chief still incorporates Dunderave in his title.

The clan fortunes had improved by the time its chief, Alexander, was knighted by James IV, only to die soon after at Flodden. The clan stayed loyal to the Stewarts, and young Macnachten rode, resplendent in shining armour, at the head of his clansmen to join Dundee at the Battle of Killiecrankie. But just before the 1715 Jacobite rising the Loch Fyne lands passed to the Campbells in payment for debts.

There is an almost Biblical flavour about the wedding, in 1700, of one of the last of the Scottish-based chiefs. He was to marry the daughter of Sir James Campbell of Ardkinglas but, having been well plied with drink, he woke up the next day to find himself married not to the second daughter, the one of his choice, but to her elder sister. Macnachten and the second daughter fled to Ireland, leaving his wife to give birth to a daughter which her father drowned in the river. The father-in-law then had Macnachten condemned for incest and was rewarded with his lands.

The clan motto is "I hope in God" and the badge is a castle.

TARTAN The Macnachten tartan has a red background with symmetrically arranged green and black squares. It closely resembles the MacDuff, which may bear out the claim that the Macnachtens were originally a Moray tribe transplanted by Malcolm IV.

There are many septs of this clan, including the various spellings of the name, such as Macnaughton and Macnaughtan.

The most telling story about the MacNeils of Barra, one-time owners of that idyllic Hebridean island, is a true and proper tale that indicates their place in the scheme of things and their own judgement of their status. When the MacNeil of Barra had dined in his island fastness, Kisimul Castle, his trumpeters were sent to the battlements to announce to the whole world: "Hear, O ye people, and listen, O ye nations! The MacNeil of Barra having finished his meal, the princes of the earth may dine."

Of such is the confidence of chiefs and the ancient glory of the clan. But then the MacNeils are descended from the Irish High King, Niall of the Nine Hostages. Tradition has it that Niall, a grandson of the last Irish King of this line, settled in Barra in about 1040 and founded the Scottish clan of Niall or MacNeil.

But it was not until 1427 that a formal charter for Barra was granted by David II to Gilleonan MacNeil, 9th chief of Barra, ranking the MacNeils as Barons in the Kingdom of the Lords of the Isles. Even after the power of the Lords of the Isles had been broken by the King the MacNeils of Barra and those of that other Hebridean island, Gigha, kept their island territories, though the Barra MacNeils followed the Macleans of Duart, while the Gigha MacNeils sided with the MacDonalds of Islay.

But both still had independent power and dominion. When Rory the Turbulent, chief of the Barra MacNeils, whose raiding longboats sailed as far as the Irish coast, was accused of harassing English shipping, his bold retort to James VI, son of Mary, Queen of Scots, was that he considered he was doing a service by annoying the woman who had killed the King's mother.

As well as being proud and mighty the MacNeil chiefs also ran their own very personal social service. They found wives and husbands for those who had been widowed, took the elderly poor into their own household and replaced crofters' cows which had died.

This island race established other outposts, on the islands of Oronsay and Colonsay, the latter of which became the seat of the clan for a while. In the 16th century, as the power of the Campbells increased, that of the MacNeils declined, apart from Barra, where they were insulated against the slings and arrows of clan fortunes. Gigha had a more chequered history. Its last chief, Neil, was killed in battle in 1530 and in 1544 the island was sold to James MacDonald of Islay. Later bought back, the Gigha estates came into the possession of the MacNeils of Colonsay.

The MacNeils became involved in supporting the Stewart cause, the MacNeil of Barra rallying to Dundee's rising and described as "panting under the weight of a great battle-axe" as he led many of his young men into battle. By the time of the Jacobite risings in the 18th century the clan was less prominent, though a Spanish ship landed arms and money at Barra for the Prince's army.

Though the MacNeil chief did not take part in the 1745 rising, he had the problem of a local minister who sent off despatches telling the government that Bonnie Prince Charlie was on Barra. Fortunately no one believed him and the Prince escaped, but MacNeil was still imprisoned, and came close to losing his lands.

The chief's son, known as Roderick the Peaceful, was killed at the storming of Quebec in 1759, and his grandson, the next (20th) chief, Colonel Roderick, moved from Kisimul to a house on Barra. When he died in 1822 the direct male line ended with his son, who had been an officer at Waterloo and who had to sell Barra in 1838. Many MacNeils emigrated to America at the time of the Highland clearances.

After 700 years of occupancy Kisimul Castle was left to the mercy of wind and weather until in 1937 a descendant of one of those emigrants, Robert Lister MacNeil, an American architect, bought back a large chunk of Barra and the castle, which he restored. Robert MacNeil was the great-grandson of the 22nd chief, and he himself became the 25th chief, his title confirmed by the Lyon court in 1915.

The present, 26th chief of the clan is Robert MacNeil's Harvard-educated son, Professor Ian Roderick MacNeil of Barra, a Professor of Law at Northwestern University, whose home is at 3500 North Lake Shore Drive, Chicago.

Colonsay, the other MacNeil island, remained in the clan until, on the death of Sir James MacNeil, V.C. it was sold to Lord Strathcona in 1904. After the death of Alexander MacNeil, the chiefship passed to his son, also Alexander, whose home was in New Zealand. Many branches of the clan also settled in Northern Ireland. The MacNeils were at one time hereditary harpists and pipers to the Macleans of Duart.

The clan motto of the MacNeil of Barra is *Vincere vel mori* — "To conquer or die" — and the badge is a rock.

TARTAN There are five MacNeil tartans including this one, the MacNeil of Colonsay. The oldest sett has a simple green background and black and red checks.

Septs include MacGougan, MacGrail, MacNeal, MacNelly, Neil and Nelson.

Since the Celtic church did not have a celibate priesthood, the Macphersons are yet another clan whose name derives from ecclesiastical origins. Like the MacNabs ("son of the Abbot") and the MacTaggarts ("son of the priest") Macpherson means "son of the parson". The founder is said to be Ewan Ban, son of Duncan, who was the 12th-century prior (or parson) at Kingussie. The neighbouring Inverness-shire town of Newton-more today houses the pioneering Clan Macpherson Museum, established in the 1950s and the first such to be devoted entirely to a clan's history. Cluny Castle, once the seat of the chief, has been sold but the clan still owns some of its heartland in Badenoch.

Clan Macpherson was one of the most important members of the clan Chattan confederation of clans, and for many years it was arguing their right, rather than that of the Mackintoshes, to be the leaders of Chattan. They based their claim on the fact that Dougal, the 6th chief of clan Chattan, and the descendant of Ewan Ban's son Gilli-chattan, had a daughter Eva, heiress of the clan, who married Angus Mackintosh. From this marriage descend the chiefs of the clan Chattan, but the Lord Lyon ruled in the 17th century that the chiefship had passed through Eva to the Mackintoshes.

Clan Macpherson is also known as the "clan of the three brothers", the sons of the founders of Ewen Ban. These were Kenneth, the founder of the famous line of Cluny-Macpherson, John, ancestor of the Pitmain branch, and Gillies of Invereshie. Sir Aeneas Macpherson of Invereshie, who was born in 1644 and became a lawyer, was the first clan historian. He also lived dangerously, working as a Jacobite agent under the alias of Williamson, which did not prevent his being detected and imprisoned in England in 1690. Finally, after being in and out of prison several times, he was banished and went to the Jacobite court in St. Germain, though eventually, in 1702, he was allowed to return home.

The head of the clan was the Cluny-Macpherson line, whose most outstanding chief was Ewen Macpherson of Cluny, the son-in-law of Lord Lovat, who succeeded at the time of the '45. He mustered 600 clansmen to fight for Bonnie Prince Charlie and proved himself a gallant fighter, though he was not able to reach Culloden in time for that final battle. What he did manage was to help the Prince to escape, for which his house of Cluny was burnt to the ground and he was outlawed. Even with the then enormous price of £1,000 on his head he managed to hide out on his Badenoch lands with the help of his clansmen for nine years, eventually escaping to France in 1755. The Cluny estates were forfeited, but were eventually restored to Ewen's son, Duncan, in 1784.

Duncan's son, Ewen, known as "Old Cluny", lived in pictu-resque style as a Highland chief until his death in 1885. He was succeeded by three of his sons in turn, but on the death of the youngest, Albert Cameron, the estate, including Cluny Castle, was sold, while the title passed to his nephew, Ewen of Cluny Macpherson, the 18th chief, who lived in Adelaide, Australia. He died in 1966, and a cousin, Brigadier Alan Macpherson, suc-ceeded. The present chief is his son, barrister Sir William Macpherson of Cluny-Macpherson, who lives at Newton of Blairgowrie, Perthshire.

The clan motto is that of clan Chattan, "Touch not the cat without a glove", and the badge is a cat. There are two plant badges, boxwood and white heather.

TARTAN There are five Macpherson tartans, one hunting and two clan tartans, one belonging to the chief and one known as the Cluny tartan. Even the two clan tartans are elaborate enough to belong to a chief, and are thought to be a mixture of the Royal Stewart and the MacDuff designs. They are both red tartans, unlike this the hunting tartan, which has a grey back-ground. "Old Cluny", who lived in high style as a 19th-century Highland chief, said that this clan design, known as the *Breacan Glas* (the grey hunting plaid of Badenoch) had been used and beloved by the clan long before the Jacobite Stewarts had been heard of in Scotland. Its sett was copied from an old plaid at Cluny by Jean, wife of the celebrated Jacobite, Ewen Cluny of Macpherson, and the daughter of Lord Lovat. The design of the chief's tartan closely resembles that of the Mack-intosh Chief, leader of the clan Chattan.

From their tiny clan territory on the island of Ulva, which measures only 5 miles by 2½, off the coast of Mull, the MacQuarries have spread themselves throughout the world, gaining distinction out of all proportion to their numbers. Nowadays there is more clan interest overseas — in Nova Scotia, America and Australia, the last recognizing Lachlan MacQuarrie as one of its founding fathers — than in Scotland, where the last known chief died in 1818.

Though the smallest of Highland clans, the MacQuarries had a place of honour as an ancient tribe in the councils of the Lords of the Isles. Their name expresses the esteem in which they were held, deriving from that of the royal Prince, *Guaire*, meaning "noble", who was the brother of Fingon, founder of the Mackinnon clan. The Macguires or Macguaires of Ireland are related through Gregor, second son of Cormac Mor, the chief of the MacQuarries, who was killed by Norsemen during the 13th-century reign of King Alexander II.

Most of the MacQuarrie family papers were destroyed in a fire in 1688, so early records are sparse. But we know that after the downfall of the Lord of the Isles the MacQuarries aligned themselves with their powerful island neighbours, the Macleans of Duart, on Mull. This involved them in following the Macleans in what proved to be a disaster from which the clan never really recovered, the loss of their chief and most of his clansmen at the battle of Inverkeithing in 1651.

There was still a chief on Ulva when Dr. Johnson and James Boswell visited Lachlan MacQuarrie, "an intelligent, polite man of the world", in 1773. He also owned the island of Staffa, with its famous Fingal's Cave, immortalized in music by Mendelssohn.

The most famous McQuarrie soldier was the chief's cousin, another Lachlan, who was born on Ulva, became a Major-General and was appointed Governor of New South Wales. When this Scot, who shares with Macarthur the title "Father of Australia", retired in 1821, he bought himself an estate on Mull and remained there until his death in 1824.

The clan motto is *An t'Arm breac dearg* which means "the red-tartaned army". The badge is a mailed arm rising out of a crown and holding a dagger.

TARTAN There are four MacQuarrie tartans, all with red backgrounds. This is the most common one; it is related to the red MacDonald. Septs are simply variations of the name, including Wharrie and MacGorry.

The clan Macqueen, or MacSween (there are various spellings, including MacSwan), is said to be of Norse origin, the name deriving from the Scandinavian name, Sweyn. Like their Viking ancestors the Hebridean MacSweens, particularly the modern men of Scalpay, have the reputation of being great seafarers. At Garafadon, on Skye, the Macqueens held lands for many centuries, evidently on condition that they paid their rent in salmon. But during the 1800s many of the clan emigrated, particularly across the Atlantic, though Donald, the last known chief, who succeeded in 1896, went to New Zealand. Nothing has been heard of his line since.

Though they are mainly a Hebridean and west Highland clan, there were MacSweens living in Argyllshire in the 13th century, their base the mighty Castle Sween on Loch Sween. The castle, built in the mid-12th century and thought to be the oldest on the Scottish mainland, was destroyed by Montrose's troops in 1647.

There is another mention of mainland members, this time the Macqueens, in the early 15th century, when a MacDonald bride from Moidart married Malcolm, 10th chief of the Mackintoshes. Several of the Macqueen clan, who were followers of the MacDonalds of Clanranald, accompanied her and stayed to become a sept of the clan Chattan. One of these was Revan Macqueen, who fought under Mackintosh at the battle of Harlaw in 1411, and from whom his descendants, who settled at Corrybrough on the river Findhorn, Inverness-shire, took the name of the clan Revan.

These Macqueens seem to have lost their Corrybrough lands towards the end of the 18th century. When the chief, John Fraser Macqueen, died in 1881 the title went to his brother Lachlan, a distinguished officer in the East India Company. His son, Donald, who emigrated to New Zealand, was the last known chief.

The clan motto is "Constant and faithful" and the badge is a wolf rampant holding an arrow.

TARTAN The Macqueen tartan has a red background with black checks and a yellow stripe, a reversal of the MacKeane tartan.

Septs are variations on the name, including MacWhan, Revans and Swan.

· MACRAE ·

The Macraes are another clan with origins in the Celtic church. In Gaelic *MacRath* means "son of grace" and there are many English spellings of it, such as Macra, Macraw and Macraith. But the Irish form of the name, Macgrath, is the one said most closely to resemble the original pronunciation. Macraes are found scattered all over Scotland, for the name was also a commonly-used Christian name there and in Ireland in early times.

The story-book Castle of Eilean Donan, picturesquely sited on a rocky islet at the meeting place near Skye of three sea lochs — Duich, Alsh and Long — is closely connected with the Macraes, who became its keepers. Named after St. Donnan, martyred on the island of Eigg, it was built by King Alexander II in the 13th century on the site of an old fort as a defence against the Norse sea raiders.

Eilean Donan became a stronghold of the Mackenzies of Kintail, whom the Macraes faithfully supported — as bodyguards they were called "Mackenzie's coat of mail" — and from 1520 onwards the Macraes were keepers of the castle. It was an arrow fired by Duncan Macrae, 5th chief of Kintail, that fatally wounded the chief of the MacDonalds of Sleat when he besieged the castle in 1539 in his unsuccessful attempt to restore the Lordship of the Isles.

Some twenty years later the same Duncan was granted the lands of Inverinate, on Loch Duich (now part of a state forest), which remained in the clan for more than 200 years. In the 17th century the Reverend Farquhar Macrae was keeper of Eilean Donan as well as vicar of Kintail for 44 years, and one of his sons, the Reverend John Macrae of Dingwall, founded the line of the Macraes of Conchra.

The Macrae warriors earned themselves the title of the "wild Macraes" when the large numbers who had joined the Seaforth Highlanders — the regiment founded in 1778 by the Mackenzie chief, the Earl of Seaforth — mutinied because they thought they were not going to get fair treatment. Four years earlier, John Macrae of Kintail had emigrated to America, joining the losing side in the War of Independence. Before dying as a prisoner he composed Gaelic songs that survived him and are still remembered in Kintail.

The Lord Lyon was asked in 1909 to recognize Sir Colin Macrae of Inverinate as the chief, but his claim was challenged by a Macrae of Conchra, and the question of the chiefship has not yet been settled. But Eilean Donan Castle — blown up by an English frigate bombarding Spanish mercenaries quartered there during the abortive 1715 Jacobite rebellion — has been restored by a descendant of its Macrae keepers. Lt. Colonel John Macrae-Gilstrap of Balliemore, of the Conchra branch, bought the ruin and turned it into his home in 1932. His son, Captain John Macrae, succeeded him and the castle is now open to the public.

The clan motto of the Macraes of Inverinate is *Fortitudine* — "With fortitude" — and the badge is a hand holding a sword.

TARTAN There are four versions of the Macrae tartan, two being hunting designs, and this one, called "the Prince's own", is the red tartan that was named in 1745 for the personal use of Bonnie Prince Charlie and is certainly an old Macrae pattern. It is not known if it was worn earlier or merely adopted later as a tribute to the Prince. While the Macraes had fought valiantly and lost many men in the Jacobite army at Sheriffmuir in 1715, they were not out as a clan in the '45, though many individual clansmen took part. One of the hunting tartans is known as the Macrae Sheriffmuir tartan. The fourth tartan, sometimes called dress Macrae, is said to be devised from the tartan worn by some of the clan in battle.

The septs of the Macraes are principally spelling variations of the name, ranging from Macara to Maccreath, Maccraw and Machray, as well as Ray and Reath.

The clan *MacMathan* in Gaelic, Macmahon in Irish, and Matheson in English — sometimes called Clan of the Bear — was originally part of the ancient Celtic Earldom of Ross. Though their early history is obscure it is known that their clan lands were at Lochalsh and that they were once as powerful as the clan Mackenzie — able, like them, to summon 2,000 clansmen to arms — and were the keepers of Eilean Donan Castle before the Macraes. As the power of the Lords of the Isles declined in the 16th century that of the Mackenzies and Macleods increased, while the Mathesons, squeezed between two such ambitious feuding neighbours, almost sank from sight for nearly 200 years.

Their fortunes were spectacularly revived in Victorian times by two clansmen from the Sutherland branch of Shiness, who made fortunes in the East and returned to reclaim the clan lands that had been sold off.

Alexander Matheson, whose father, John, the 4th chief of Attadale, in Ross-shire, had reunited the two main branches of the clan, by marrying Margaret, daughter of the chief of the Shiness Mathesons, joined his uncle, James Matheson, in the India and China trade.

James was a founder of the famous Far Eastern company, Jardine, Matheson, and the two each made enough money to buy large chunks of Scotland. James Matheson bought most of the island of Lewis in 1844, including the former castle of the Macleods at Stornoway, and was later knighted. Alexander, whose father had been forced to sell the Attadale estate, reclaimed 220,000 acres in Ross-shire at a cost of nearly £800,000 and became the 1st Baronet of Lochalsh in 1882.

The present chief is Major Sir Torquhil Matheson of Matheson, the 6th Baronet of Lochalsh, who lives in Somerset. His father, confirmed as chief of the clan Matheson by the Lord Lyon in 1963, is a descendant of the Mathesons of Bennetsfield, in the Black Isle, Ross-shire, a property originally acquired in 1688 on the proceeds of cattle-droving.

The clan motto of the Mathesons of Lochalsh is *Fac et spera* — "Do and hope". The badge is an arm holding a sword, rising out of a crown.

TARTAN There are three Matheson tartans, one of which is a more modern hunting tartan. This is the most commonly worn one, red with green and black checks, and is thought to be made up from two or more other tartans, one of which may be the Erskine.

The Maxwells are a Border clan, one of the very powerful families who reigned in that turbulent area when it was fought over by the Scots and the English. Many branches spread throughout Scotland, but of most interest today are the relics of the clan's past wealth and grandeur. These include Pollok estate in Glasgow, given to the city by the Stirling-Maxwells and now the home of the world-famous Burrell Museum. Picturesque Traquair House, Peebles-shire, still the home of the Maxwell-Stuart family, dates back at least seven centuries and is the oldest inhabited house in Scotland. Its famous main gates, closed since the '45, are not to be re-opened until there is a Stewart king on the throne, underlining the Maxwells' centuries of political involvement and commitment to the Scottish crown. It is open to the public.

The Maxwells' great Castle of Caerlaverock, built in the early 1200s in a commanding position on the Solway Firth, south of Dumfries, was first occupied by Sir John Maxwell, Lord Chamberlain of Scotland, in around 1230.

The 8th Lord Maxwell rose to become the Earl of Morton in 1581, after the holder of that title, a member of that other powerful Border family, the Douglases, had been executed in Edinburgh. But the title was later given back to the Douglases and, in recompense, the Maxwells were made Earls of Nithsdale in the 17th century.

The most famous Nithsdale is the 5th Earl, who, after joining the Jacobite rising of 1715, was sentenced to death for high treason in Westminster Hall. His resourceful wife smuggled women's clothing into the Tower of London and he escaped dressed as her maid. The Nithsdales fled to the Jacobite court in Rome, where they lived in poverty.

In 1858, Winifred's grandson, who changed his name to William Constable-Maxwell, proved his claim to the subsidiary Nithsdale title of the Lordship of Terregles. When his son died in 1908 the title passed to his daughter, who had married the Duke of Norfolk. The present, 14th holder of this Scottish lordship of Herries of Terregles is also a woman. Lady Anne, eldest daughter of the late Duke of Norfolk, inherited it — the only title not to pass to the succeeding Duke of Norfolk — through her grandmother. William Maxwell of Corruchan established a claim as the male heir of the Maxwells in the Lyon court.

The clan motto of the house of Corruchan is *Reviresco* — "I flourish again". The badge is a stag standing in front of a holly bush.

TARTAN This red and green checked tartan is a Lowland one.

The Menzies of Menzies, present chief of the clan, now lives in Dalkeith, Western Australia, where another clansman, Sir Robert Menzies, who was made a Knight of the Thistle by the Queen, rose to prominence as Prime Minister. The Clan Menzies Society in Scotland is still very active, having bought back the centuries-old chief's seat, Castle Menzies, and restored it as a clan museum and centre.

There are two schools of thought about the clan's name; one is that it denotes a Gaelic race and the other, more likely, is that it is from the Norman place-name, Mesnières, later to be translated into Meyneris, the surname of the Norman administrator first recorded as Lord Chamberlain of Scotland in 1249. The name itself has a variety of pronunciations and forms, "Mingus" being the more common Scottish way.

In the 13th century the Menzies were granted lands in Strath Tay, where many of the clan still live. A David Menzies became Governor of Orkney in the 15th century under its Norwegian rulers, and in the civil wars of the 17th century Menzies were to be found serving both sides. The only slight contretemps in which they appear to have been involved was when their castle at Weems was burnt down in 1503 after a quarrel with their neighbours, the Stewarts of Fortingall. It was rebuilt shortly afterwards and was firmly renamed Castle Menzies after Sir Robert Menzies had his lands made into a barony by James V.

Sir Alexander Menzies of Menzies was made a Baronet of Nova Scotia in 1665, and this line continued until this century, when the 8th Baronet, Sir Neil, died without an heir in 1910 and his sister, Egidia, was chieftainess until her death. In 1957 Ronald Menzies, of the Culdares branch, was recognized as chief by the Lord Lyon. The clan motto is *Vil God I Zal*—"Will God I shall" — and the badge is a savage's head.

TARTAN There are five Menzies tartans, and three of the setts are identical apart from their colourings. This attractive red-and-green hunting tartan drew admiring comments from Queen Victoria when she first saw it.

Septs include MacMinn, MacMonies, Mein, Mengues and Minnus.

The Montgomerys (or Montgomeries) are a Lowland clan of Norman origin. The Montgomerys who moved to Scotland became the Earls of Eglinton in 1507, after marrying into that Scottish family. The present chief of the clan is Archibald, the 18th Earl of Eglinton, who lives in Hampshire. Originally the clan lands were at Eaglesham, Renfrewshire. The first to make his mark was John Montgomery, who captured Harry Hotspur at the Battle of Otterburn in 1338; with the ransom he received he built the fine Castle of Polnoon on his estate. He added lands at Ardrossan by marrying the heiress of Sir Hugh Eglinton, and their grandson became the 1st Lord Montgomerie (the spelling the family still use for the heir to the title) and Ambassador to England.

A later Earl of Eglinton, the 4th, died violently in 1586, murdered by his neighbours, the Cunninghames, in a feud that lasted for a century. His son Hugh, the 5th Earl, died without an heir, and the title passed, despite the disapproval voiced by the King, to Sir Alexander Seton, who had married the 3rd Earl's daughter.

Sir Alexander's son, the 7th Earl, also Alexander, was a staunch Covenanter who was imprisoned by General Monk in 1659 for his support of Charles II. The 9th Earl furthered the family fortunes by adding several estates in Ayrshire, and by fathering large numbers of children through his three marriages. His last marriage was to the beautiful and talented Susannah, six feet tall and fair-complexioned, the daughter of Kennedy of Culzean, in Ayrshire, to whom Allan Ramsay dedicated *The Gentle Shepherd*. Though he was twice her age, Susannah chose the Earl in preference to many younger suitors and bore him seven beautiful daughters, each as tall and graceful as herself. By his three Countesses the Earl had a dozen daughters and, desperate for a male heir, threatened to divorce Susannah. She spiritedly retorted that he could do so, but he must first restore her youth, her beauty and her virginity.

Susannah did go on to have sons, and they became the 10th and the 11th Earls, the last of the direct line.

The clan motto is *Gardez bien*—"Look well"—and the badge is a female holding an anchor in her right hand and a savage's head in her left.

TARTAN This unusual tartan has probably been used by the clan since the Union of Scotland and England in 1707, which would make it one of the earliest of the Lowland tartans. Their other tartan has a plain green background with blue stripes.

The clan Morrison settled mainly on the long Hebridean island that divides into Lewis and Harris, but how and when they arrived there is uncertain. Two speculative derivations of the name — both Gaelic — suggest different origins. The first is that they are descended from northern Irish bards, the *O'Muircheasain*. The second, and more probable, is that they had connections with the Celtic church, since *Mac Ghille Mhuire* means "son of the Virgin Mary's servant".

Romantic legend, too, has it that a Norse family of Morrisons, that of the natural son of the King of Norway, was shipwrecked on Lewis, floating ashore on driftwood. The story is commemorated in their plant badge, a piece of driftwood. (Many clans have plant badges in addition to official badges; they are believed to be lucky charms rather than a means of identification.) Whatever the truth, the Morrisons settled at the north end of Lewis, around Ness, and by the 19th century they totalled 1400 people, a sizeable proportion of the population.

While the Morrisons of Harris farmed, including the islands of Pabbay, Bernera and Taransay, the Morrisons of Lewis held the hereditary legal office of brieve or judge to the Macleods, Hugh Morrison, in the 16th century, being the first to be mentioned. But their legal duties ended once James VI instructed the mainland clans to "extirpate the barbarous peoples of the isles", and many of the clan moved across the Minch to settle in Durness, Sutherland, the Mackays' country. One explanation of this move, evidently of as many as 60 families, is that they accompanied their chief when he married a daughter of the Bishop of Caithness.

A modern-day Morrison, whose ancestors came from North Uist, was speaker of the House of Commons in the 1950s, became Viscount Dunrossil, and was Governor-General of Australia. His elder brother was judged chief of the clan by the Lord Lyon in 1967. His son, Ian, a physician like his father, is now the chief and lives in Sussex. Lord Margadale is head of the Islay branch of the Morrisons.

The clan motto is "Castle Eistein" and the badge a castle rising from the sea, with a hand holding a dagger emerging from it.

TARTAN This green and black Morrison tartan is a fairly late one, and is the same as that of the Mackay, but with the addition of a red stripe. Another Morrison tartan with a red background, evidently copied from the tartan covering of an old family bible, was registered with the Lyon Court in 1968.

There have been Munros of Foulis, in Ross-shire, since the 12th century, and Captain Patrick Munro of Foulis, the 33rd chief of the clan, still lives at Foulis Castle, near Dingwall. Yet despite this continuity and documentary evidence going back over 600 years, the exact origins of *Clann Rothaich* are uncertain. One suggestion has been that they were the *Monrosse* or "mountain men" of Ross-shire. Another is that they are of Irish origin, from the river Roe, in Derry, and indeed there is still an Irish branch of the clan, descended from the Munros of Kiltearn.

The first chief to be mentioned, Hugh of Foulis, lived in the 12th century, and by the beginning of the next century George Munro of Foulis had got a legal title to his Ross-shire lands from the Earl of Sutherland. By 1309 Robert Munro, who fought for Bruce at Bannockburn, had been granted more lands in Strathspey, while a later Robert was influential enough to marry a niece of the Queen.

Throughout the following centuries the Munros made their marks as military men, particularly in the continental wars, and in the New World as politicians rising to high office. The most famous was James Monroe, President of the United States from 1817 to 1825, who enshrined the clan name in his Monroe Doctrine. A descendant of another Munro, who had been transported to New England in 1651 after the defeat of the Royalists, was Ebenezer Munro, one of the Lexington minutemen, who claimed to have fired the first shot in the American War of Independence in 1775. The Scottish Munros also fired many shots, particularly in the 17th-century Thirty Years War in Europe. The 18th clan chief, Robert Munro, nicknamed "the Black Baron", went to Sweden with the Mackay regiment in 1626 and joined the army of King Gustavus Adolphus. He became a Colonel of two Dutch regiments and was killed by a musket ball and buried at Ulm.

When Sir Hector, the 11th Baronet, died in 1935 the chiefship passed for the first time to a woman. His eldest daughter, Mrs. Eva Gascoigne, inherited Foulis Castle and became known as the 32nd Lady of Foulis, while the Baronetcy passed to a cousin.

The clan motto is "Dread God" and its badge is an eagle .

TARTAN This, the Munro dress tartan, has a red background with a complex design of stripes and checks. The Munros use the 42nd Black Watch tartan as their hunting tartan.

Septs of the clan include Dingwall, Fowlis, Keddie, MacCulloch, Monro and Vass.

The chief of the great clan Murray, the Duke of Atholl, still has his own army of Atholl Highlanders, the only private army allowed in Britain. But nowadays the Duke's marshalling of his troops is for ceremony rather than conquest. It has helped to make the clan seat, turretted Blair Castle, at Blair Atholl, near Pitlochry, full of family history, one of Scotland's prime tourist attractions.

Romantic relics of Bonnie Prince Charlie recall the clan's great general, Lord George Murray, who masterminded the Jacobite army's march on London, but had to order the retreat from Derby. His elder brother, the Marquess of Tullibardine, unfurled the Prince's standard at Glenfinnan, while another clan member, John Murray of Broughton, landed with the Prince at Moidart as his secretary. After Culloden he is said to have buried huge sums of gold, which have never been unearthed, near Loch Askaig.

The Murrays, descendants of the ancient *mormaers*, or nobles, of Moray, the land from which their name comes, have down the centuries been in the forefront of Scotland's struggles for independence from the English. The first great freedom fighter was Sir Andrew Murray of Bothwell, whose father had died a prisoner in the Tower of London and who was one of the first to join Sir William Wallace when he raised his standard against Edward I of England in the 13th century. It was his son, also Sir Andrew, who in 1297 sent the triumphant letter to the Mayors of Lubeck and Hamburg announcing that Scotland had been liberated and that the Scottish ports were open for trade. After Bruce's death he became Regent of Scotland.

The 1st Duke of Atholl, ennobled by Queen Anne in 1703, and whose sons were to become the Jacobite leaders, was so vehemently opposed to the 1707 Union of Scotland and England that he called out 4,000 armed troops.

The Murrays, apart from their feudal base in Morayshire, acquired great possessions through prudent marriages, starting with the lands of Tullibardine, near Crieff, in the 14th century, of which they became Earls in 1606. William, the 2nd Earl of Tullibardine, married the even wealthier heiress of the 5th Earl of Atholl, and their son, John, took the Atholl title in 1629, while their grandson became a Marquess in 1676.

An even greater prize, the Isle of Man, came the way of the 2nd Duke of Atholl, through his mother. When the 3rd Duke gave up its sovereignty to the British Crown in 1765 it was valued at £70,000 plus an annual pension of £4,000.

Other branches of the clan established separate dynasties. Sir David Murray, who foiled the Gowrie conspiracy, the plot to murder James VI in 1600, was rewarded with the Gowries' abbey lands of Scone, and his descendants, first created Viscounts Stormont, are now the Earls of Mansfield, who live in Scone Palace. Another younger son, Patrick Murray, founded the house of Ochtertyre, in Perthshire, which became a Baronetcy in 1673. Other Murray titles included the Earls of Dysart and of Dunmore, and in the south of Scotland they became the Earls of Annandale.

The clan motto is *Tout prêt* — "Quite ready" — and the badge is a mermaid holding a mirror in one hand and a comb in the other.

TARTAN The Murray of Atholl tartan is the simplest, and probably therefore the oldest, of the three Murray tartans, and is also the design used by the Murrays of Mansfield.

The red Murray of Tullibardine tartan is said to have been first worn by Charles, second son of the 1st Marquis of Tullibardine, who was made Earl of Dunmore and was colonel in 1679 of the Royal Grey Dragoons, later the Royal Scots Greys. The general Murray tartan was once a district tartan and may have been the Atholl tartan before being renamed.

Septs include Balneaves, Dunbar, Dunsmore, Neaves, Piper, Small and Spalding.

The lovely but remote Angus glens of Glenisla, Glenprosen and Glenclova are the heartland of the "Bonnie Hoose o'Airlie", the chiefs of the clan Ogilvie, who take their name from the barony of Ogilvy, near Glamis, lands granted to them in 1127. Glamis Castle was, of course, the childhood home of the Queen Mother, Lady Elizabeth Bowes-Lyon, and a royal bride also married into the Ogilvie clan when Princess Alexandra, daughter of the late Duke of Kent, became the wife of Angus Ogilvy, second son of the 12th Earl of Airlie. Their children, James and Marina Ogilvy, are in line to the British throne.

The 13th Earl of Airlie, the present Ogilvy chief, has his seat at Cortachy Castle, Kirriemuir, Angus. Airlie Castle, the "Bonnie Hoose" of the ballad, sited on a rocky promontory north-east of Alyth, Angus, was one of the proudest and most massive fortresses in central Scotland and had been the home of the Earls since 1431. But it was sacked in 1640 by the Campbells when the 1st Earl was away in England, supporting the Stewart cause of Charles I.

"The lady looked over her window sae high,
An' O, but she grat sairly,
To see Argyll an' a his men
Come to plunder the bonnie hoose o' Airlie."

The lady Ogilvy, according to the ballad, spiritedly tells the false Argyll that if her good lord had been there instead of with Charlie neither Argyll nor any other Scottish lord would have dared set foot on the lands of Airlie, and that she would give all her 11 bonnie sons to fight for Charlie.

The Ogilvies were thereafter steadfastly loyal to the Stewart cause. The 2nd Earl was captured in 1645 after Montrose had been defeated at Philiphaugh, and was condemned to death. But on the eve of his execution his sister helped him to escape dressed in her clothes. His descendants were equally blessed with good luck when, after the young son of the 4th Earl had raised the clan in the '45, after Culloden he managed to escape to France. David, Lord Ogilvy, was barely 20 years old when he joined Bonnie Prince Charlie. He was attainted, and after reaching France he joined the French army and rose to become a Lieutenant-General. He succeeded on his father's death in 1761 and was eventually pardoned, in 1778, because of his extreme youth at the time of the '45. The Earldom was finally restored to his grandson, the 7th Earl, in 1826. The 8th Earl of Airlie was killed in 1900 while leading his regiment in a charge at the South African Battle of Diamond Hill.

The Ogilvy clan also became prominent in the north-east, where other branches were given the titles of the Earls of Findlater and of Seafield, as well as Lords of Banff, a title which became dormant in 1803. James, the second son of the 3rd Earl of Findlater, who was created Earl of Seafield in 1701, is remembered for his infamous part in pushing through the Act of Union in 1707 and for his remark, "There's the end of an auld sang" as it was signed and sealed. The title of Earl of Findlater became dormant in 1811, while the Seafield title was inherited by the Grants.

David, the 13th Earl of Ogilvie and the present chief, married Virginia Ryan, daughter of John Ryan, of Newport, Rhode Island, USA, and they have three sons and three daughters.

The clan motto is *A Fin* — "To the end" — and the badge is a naked woman holding a portcullis.

TARTAN This tartan, now known as the Ogilvy, is one of the most complex. It has carried the Ogilvie name only since 1812, having previously been known as the Drummond of Strathallan. Before that there was an older, much simpler Ogilvie tartan. The green and blue Ogilvie hunting tartan may be older than either of these two.

Septs include Findlater, Gilchrist, Richardson and Storey.

The head of the clan Robertson is always styled Struan Robertson, after its namesake, Robert Riach (Grizzled Robert), whose lands of Struan were erected into a barony in 1451. It was his reward for capturing the murderers of James I, and thereafter his was the name his kinsmen took.

But the clan is almost as well known, under his grandfather's Gaelic name, as *Clann Donnachaidh*. Donnachaidh Reamhar, "Stout Duncan", was a sturdy friend of Robert the Bruce and led the clan into battle for him at Bannockburn. Duncan was descended from the Celtic Earls of Atholl.

Dunalastair, near Tummel Bridge, and Struan, near Blair Atholl, are the burial sites of the clan. It is now landless, but its history is carefully documented at the Clan Donnachaidh Museum, which was opened in 1969 at Bruar Falls, west of Blair Atholl. Here the famous *Clach na Brataich*, the charm-stone which has been linked with the clan's fortunes since Bannockburn, has pride of place. It was the clan's unswerving loyalty to the Stewart cause that was eventually to lead to the loss of its great territories.

In 1749 Margaret became the 18th chief, but the estates were seized by the government from the 19th chief, her cousin. Though dispossessed, the chiefs of Struan lived on at Loch Rannoch, latterly in Rannoch Barracks, which had been built to house the Hanoverian troops after the '45, but was later converted into a residence.

In 1910 Miss Jean Rosine Robertson succeeded her brother and became the 24th chief of Struan, but within a few years the last of the clan lands had been sold. Her cousin, George Robertson of Struan, the next chief, had his arms recorded with the Lyon court. The present Robertson of Struan lives in Kent.

The senior cadet branch is Robertson of Lude, and there are many other Robertson lines, such as those of Inches, Kindeace, Auchleeks, Faskally and Blairfettie. Because of the double clan name there are numerous septs, such as Duncan or Duncanson and the Gaelic forms of that, MacConachie and MacDonachie, MacRobert and Roy.

The clan motto is *Virtutis gloria merces* — "Glory is the reward of valour" — and the badge is a hand holding an imperial crown.

TARTAN This hunting tartan, also called Robertson of Kindeace, is thought to be an old design and resembles that of the Athol Murray. There are two variants of the Robertson dress tartan. Both have red backgrounds with green and blue checks, but one, the less commonly worn, includes an additional white stripe.

This ancient clan was headed originally by the then-powerful Celtic Earldom of Ross, a title fought over by the Lords of the Isles and the Regent of Scotland. It was known to the Highlanders as *Clann Aindreas*, "the sons of Andrew", patron saint of Scotland. Some migrant Rosses made a particular mark upon American history. A Colonel George Ross was a signatory to the American Declaration of Independence, while his brother John's widow, Betsy, designed the Stars and Stripes, the first American flag.

As with so many others of the original Celtic blood, the Rosses were connected with the Celtic church, in their case through their founder, Fearchar, abbot of Applecross, and were perhaps also connected to the Irish King, Niall of the Nine Hostages. Their name was also synonymous with their lands of Ross-shire (*Ros* in Gaelic means a promontory). Fearchar Mac-an-T-Saigart ("Farquhar the priest's son") is said to have supported Alexander II against the old Celtic royal line after being disinherited by the sons of Malcolm Canmore and his Queen Margaret. For this he was made Earl of Ross in 1226.

Just over a century later the title passed through the female line into the clan Leslie, which caused a battle for supremacy, as the Lord of the Isles laid claim to this venerable title. When the Lordship itself was forfeited in 1476 the Earldom of Ross went to the crown. Meanwhile the chiefship passed to Hugh Ross of Rarinches, who had obtained a charter for his lands of Balnagowan in 1374.

For the next three centuries the Rosses of Balnagowan were the heads of the clan. Then, at the beginning of the 18th century, David Ross of Balnagowan, who had no direct heirs, settled the estate upon the Munro Rosses of Pitcalnie, near Tain.

Mr. George Ross of Pitcalnie was described on his death in 1884 at the age of 81 as the last representative of the ancient Earls of Ross. Yet again the chiefship went to a distant relative, a grand-nephew, and passed later through the female line.

The clan motto is *Spem successus alit* — "Success nourishes hope" — and the badge is a hand holding a laurel wreath.

TARTAN This Ross tartan, which has a red background with green and blue checks, has produced several variant patterns through the years. The more modern hunting tartan is principally in two shades of green.

There are many septs, including Anderson, Corbett, Dingwall, Haggart, MacCulloch, MacTaggart, MacTear, Taggart and Vass.

The Scotts, the most native-sounding of all the clans, in fact get their name from the Irish invaders who gave their name to Scotland itself. They were a powerful Border clan. The first to be mentioned in records is Uchtredus filius Scoti, who lived early in the 12th century, when he was witnessing charters. Nowadays their chief, the Duke of Buccleuch owns several stately homes which are open to the public.

The ducal title was bestowed on the bastard son of Charles II, the Duke of Monmouth, who married Anne, the Countess of Buccleuch, in 1673. The Duke was eventually beheaded; the present Buccleuchs — the name is from a remote place in the Ettrick valley — are his direct descendants.

In earlier days, before they became titled, the Scotts had been known as the "rough clan", or sometimes "the saucy Scotts", as they battled it out with their rivals, the Douglases, for control of the Border Marches.

After the fall of the Douglases the Scotts were at their peak as a clan until the Union of the Crowns in 1603.

Sir Walter Scott of Buccleuch, warden of the March of the Borders, was killed by the Kerrs in Edinburgh High Street. Despite this, there was solidarity among the Border clans, so that in 1596 the "Bold Buccleuch" was to ride to the rescue of another wild Border clansman, one of the Armstrong reivers, who had been imprisoned in England.

Sir Walter's grand-daughter, Anna, was as a child the wealthiest heiress in Scotland, even before her marriage to Charles II's natural son. Another judicious marriage brought the great Douglas of Queensberry estates into the clan possessions, plus also some English properties. So well have the Buccleuchs husbanded their estates that they still own vast tracts of Scotland stretching from Edinburgh down to the Borders and beyond.

The most famous holder of the clan name was the Edinburgh lawyer, descended from one of the leading branches of the family, Scott of Harden, who became known to the world as Sir Walter Scott, the romantic 19th-century novelist. Edinburgh's Princes Street is dominated by the monument to him, and he was the mastermind behind the tartan-bedecked 19th-century visit of George IV to Edinburgh.

The clan motto is *Amo* — "I love". The badge is a stag.

TARTAN Sir Walter Scott dismissed the idea that Border clans such as his ever had an accredited tartan. But he evidently caused this black and white checked tartan to be made for his own use. This is now ascribed to the Scotts, as is the more traditional red Scott tartan which is similar to that of the MacGregor.

Of all Scottish names, Sinclair sounds the most unquestionably Norman French. They are said to descend from St. Clair-sur-Elle, in Normandy, and first became established in Scotland around 1162 when William Sinclair was the guardian of King Alexander III's heir.

His descendants were later granted the barony of Rosslyn, near Edinburgh, where they built the beautiful little Rosslyn Chapel, rumoured even in modern times to contain the Holy Grail inside one of its magnificently carved stone pillars. A Sinclair, Sir William, had been one of those carrying the heart of Robert the Bruce to the Holy Land before he was killed fighting the Moors in Spain. Until the mid-17th century the Sinclair chiefs were buried in Rosslyn Chapel in full suits of armour.

It was in the far north of Scotland that the Sinclairs were to make their name. Henry, son of that same Sir William, became the Earl of Orkney in 1379 through marriage. His son rose to even greater heights by becoming the premier Earl of Norway, also through his wife.

This mixture of Norman, Scottish and Norse blood resulted eventually, in 1455, in the creation of an Earldom of Caithness.

Some of the Sinclairs became soldiers of fortune, Colonel George Sinclair raising a Caithness troop for the Swedish King. Ironically this band of Scottish mercenaries, kinsmen of the one-time Earl of Norway, were attacked in a narrow defile by Norwegian peasants hurling rocks and stones as they marched across Norway en route to Sweden. Many were killed and a monument marks the spot to this day.

The Earldom of Caithness has passed down through several different families of Sinclairs. Chief of the clan, the 20th Earl, Malcolm Ian Sinclair, lives in Finstock Manor, Finstock, Oxfordshire, but still has the ruins of Girnigoe Castle in Caithness. The Sinclairs of Ulster are a major branch of the clan, and it was a member of this family, Sir John Sinclair, who was the editor of the first Statistical Account of Scotland, as well as being a poet and a leading agriculturalist. He was painted by Raeburn as Commander of the Fencible regiment, which he raised in 1794.

The clan motto is "Commit thy work to God" and the badge is a cock.

TARTAN This is the Sinclair dress tartan, a red background with green and blue bands similar to that of the Menzies. The hunting tartan is a variation on this. Septs include Budge, Clyne and Lyall.

The clan Skene is said romantically to have been founded in the 11th century by a younger son of Robertson of Struan, who saved the King's life by killing a wolf with his skean (the Highlander's *sgian dhu*, or dirk, now commonly worn in the top of the stocking) and thus changed his name.

In America the name is perpetuated in Skeneborough, on Lake Champlain, founded by a clansman who was governor of the forts at Crown Point and Ticonderoga. Other Skenes also settled abroad, and one family founded an influential Austrian branch.

The lands of Skene, the other possible origin of the name, lie only a few miles west of Aberdeen, not far from the battlefield of Harlaw, where a clan chief, Adam de Skene, was killed in 1411. Two other chiefs, both called Alexander, were equally ill-fated in battle, one dying at Flodden in 1513 and his grandson at Pinkie in 1547.

James Skene of Skene was to support the Royalist cause in the time of Charles I but, like so many other Scottish clansmen, he ended up having to go abroad and fighting in foreign armies, in his case that of Gustavus Adolphus. Not much more of note is reported about the family until the 19th century, when after 500 years of male succession the direct line of the Skenes died out. That was in 1827; the estates then passed to a nephew of the last Skene of Skene, who had become the 4th Earl of Fife.

The name of Skene is also commemorated in the Skenes of Rubislaw, owners of the granite quarries that provided much of the building material for the city of Aberdeen, from whom came the family historian, Dr. William Forbes Skene, author of the *Memorials of the Family of Skene* published in 1887. Dr. Skene was also a distinguished historian of Celtic Scotland.

The chiefship of the clan probably now lies in the family of the Skenes of Hallyards, in Fife, whose descendant, Robert Skene, lives at Pitlour, Strathmiglo, Fife.

The clan motto is *Virtutis regia merces* — "A palace the reward of bravery". The badge is an arm holding a laurel wreath.

TARTAN The red and green checked Skene tartan is often called the Logan tartan, and was one of the most popular in the 19th century, when it was common to choose a tartan merely for its looks. It also bears a resemblance to the tartan of the Robertsons.

Sutherland is the name most closely linked with the infamous Highland Clearances, first practised as a planned "improvement" by the Sutherland estates in the 18th century.

The Earldom of Sutherland, created in around 1235, is said to be one of the oldest in Britain. The name is believed to come from the Norsemen's descriptive name, "the south lands", for the south-eastern parts of what is now the county of Sutherland. The founder of the clan Sutherland is said to have been Hugh, the son of William, who himself was the son of Freskin of Moray, a nobleman of Flemish origin who married into the ancient Scottish royal house.

The Earls of Sutherland, created in the 13th century, were involved in the Wars of Independence on the English side, though they later made their peace with Robert the Bruce. Indeed one later married Princess Margaret, the daughter of Robert the Bruce, though it was from another brother that the Sutherlands of Duffus, later Lords of Duffus, descended.

The Sutherlands later tangled with the Gordons, the most powerful clan and almost independent rulers of the north of Scotland in the 14th and 15th centuries. They more or less seized the Sutherland Earldom. When the 9th Earl of Sutherland died (in 1514) without a male successor, the title passed to his sister, Elizabeth, who married Adam Gordon of Aboyne, brother of the Gordon chief, the Earl of Huntly. They became the Earl and Countess of Sutherland, while their clansmen tended to adopt the surnames of either the Gordons or the Murrays.

After William, the 18th Earl, died in 1766 the title passed to his daughter, Elizabeth. She married the fabulously wealthy George Leveson-Gower, who became Marquis of Stafford and, in 1833, Duke of Sutherland. He it was who instituted the "land reforms" which forced so many Highlanders from the land of their birth and began the depopulation which is so apparent to this day.

The clan motto is *Sans peur* — "Without fear". The badge is a cat.

TARTAN There are two Sutherland tartans, the simpler of the two being identical to that of the Black Watch Highland regiment. This one also resembles the Black Watch design but has red and white lines superimposed upon it.

Septs include Chiene, Clyne, Duffus, Gray, Keith, Mowatt, Murray and Oliphant.

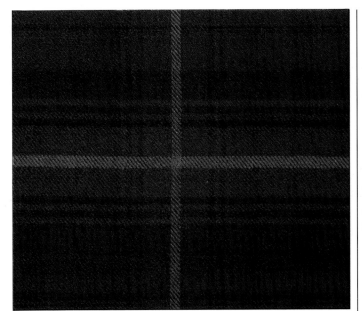

A place name is the origin of the Urquhart clan, probably a district on the north shore of the Great Glen, with a promontory overlooking Loch Ness, though some argue that the name comes from Urquhart, in the Black Isle. The first mention of it came in the 14th century, when the Urquharts were hereditary sheriffs of Cromarty and followers of the Earls of Ross, marrying into that ancient Celtic family.

Several eccentric Urquharts attracted prophecies of downfall and allegations of land-grabbing, perhaps because by the 16th century they had successfully managed to extend their possessions to include large parts of Cromarty, as well as estates in Ross-shire and Inverness-shire. Sir Thomas Urqhuart of Cromarty had another claim to fame: he fathered 25 sons, seven of whom were said to have been killed at the Battle of Pinkie in 1547.

The most renowned eccentric of the clan was Sir Thomas Urquhart, who lived from 1611 to 1660, collecting manuscripts and carrying his own works around in four trunks even as he fought for Charles II at Worcester in 1651. When he was captured the military scattered his papers in the streets and lit their pipes with his researches into a universal language. Sir Thomas was imprisoned in the Tower of London and from there he published the first work on Rabelais.

His brother's death ended the direct male line, and in 1684 the Cromarty estates were sold to Lord Tarbat, later the 1st Earl of Cromartie. But some American Urquharts — descendants of Sir Thomas's great-uncle, John, who was renowned for his natural wit and acquisitions of land and possessions — saved the clan heartlands. George Urquhart had gone to Florida in the 18th century and his son David had settled in New Orleans. In 1960 their descendants bought back the ruin of Castlecraig, on the Cromarty Firth, and Kenneth Urquhart of Urquhart, a historian who lives at 7907 Birch Street, New Orleans, Louisiana, is now chief of the clan.

The clan motto is "Mean, speak and do well", and the badge is a naked female holding a sword in her right hand and a tree in her left.

TARTAN There are three Urquhart tartans, one being very similar to that of the Black Watch but with the blue and green reversed. Another is almost identical with the Sutherland tartan. The third, shown here, has a green background, blue checks and a red stripe. It is said to have been collected in the Highlands just before King George IV's visit to Edinburgh in 1822.

This clan history ends with one of the most illustrious names in Scottish history, that of Wallace, given its glory by the famous 13th-century freedom fighter, William Wallace, who defeated the English at Stirling Bridge.

The first appearance of the name was as Wallensis, probably a medieval form used by the Celtic race of Bretons and Welsh. Richard Wallensis was a 12th-century vassal of Walter Fitzalan, the man appointed as High Steward by David I and the progenitor of Scotland's royal family of Stewart Kings. The family first settled in Ayrshire, and in the early 13th century a branch moved to Renfrewshire, starting the line from which William sprang. They had held land there for nearly a century before William Wallace was born in about 1274.

The younger son of Sir Malcolm Wallace of Elderslie, Paisley, owner of estates in Ayrshire as well as Renfrewshire, William was part of a cadet branch of the family. It was his killing of the Sheriff of Lanark in 1297 that gave the signal for the revolt against Edward I of England. After his victory at Stirling Bridge he was knighted, but in 1305 he was captured and taken to London to stand trial for treason. In his defence he argued that as he had never taken the oath of allegiance to a foreign monarch he could not be a traitor. Nevertheless he was pronounced guilty and hanged at Tyburn.

Six centuries later, monuments to him abound throughout Scotland — at his birthplace, Elderslie, at Ayr, in Lanark, at Aberdeen and, perhaps most evocative of all, at Stirling, the scene of his famous battle, where his tower is a landmark. Though the Wars of Independence continued for many years after Sir William Wallace had been hung, drawn and quartered he had lit the torch that was to illuminate the throne on which Robert the Bruce would sit.

The Wallaces of Riccarton, Craigie, Cessnock and Cairnhill are all descended from the original Wallace family of Riccarton in Ayrshire. But one family, after several generations of living in Jamaica, have emerged as the direct male descendants of the Wallaces of Riccarton, Craigie and Elderslie, home of William. The present chief of the clan is Lieutenant-Colonel Malcolm Wallace of that Ilk, who lives at Auchterarder, Perthshire.

The clan motto is *Pro Libertate* — "For liberty". The badge is a mailed arm holding a sword aloft.

TARTAN The Wallace dress tartan, with its red background, black checks and a yellow stripe, is an early example of a clan pattern. The hunting tartan, shown here, has the same pattern on a green background.

ATTAINT: Literally means to deprive of rights through a conviction for treason, or, less dramatically, to disgrace. The clan lands of attainted or declared traitors were, in fact, often forfeited to the crown. Having been annexed, they were then managed by trustees. After 1874, many of these forfeited lands were restored to their rightful owners upon the payment of sums of money, some of which were used to build Edinburgh's Register House, where all the records of Scottish births, deaths and marriages are now stored.

BOLL: A measure of weight. A boll of meal equalled 140 lbs (63.6 Kg), and was the equivalent of a payment in food to a farm-worker.

BREACAN-FEILE: The Gaelic word *Breacan* means "chequered" or "checked". *Breacan-feile* means "the belted plaid", a combination of kilt and plaid, made out of twelve ells (see ELL) of tartan, neatly pleated and fasted round the body with a belt, with the upper half thrown over the shoulder.
The *Feile-beag* (in modern Scots "PHILABEG") is the little kilt, made out of six ells of tartan, pleated and sewn, fixed at the waist with a strap, the modern way of wearing the kilt.

CLEARANCES: The Clearances occurred throughout the century or so after the Jacobites' defeat at Culloden in 1746, when the Highlanders were cleared off their lands to make way for sheep and sporting estates. Some historians claim that poverty and over-population had as large a part to play in the massive emigrations of the Highlanders to the South and overseas as land speculation. But the classic example of the Clearances was in the county of Sutherland, two-thirds owned by the Countess of Sutherland and her husband, the Marquess of Stafford, who removed about 10,000 people in the early 1800s to create sheep farms.
The most famous incident occurred when her factor, Patrick Sellar, cleared people out of Strathnaver by moving in with men and dogs and setting fire to their homes, some with old people still inside. Donald MacLeod, a Strathnaver stonemason who emigrated to Canada, wrote movingly of these times in *Gloomy Memories of the Highlands of Scotland*, while the modern author, John Prebble, has also documented this bitterly remembered period in Scottish history in his book, *The Highland Clearances*.

COVENANTERS: Charles I's insistence that the English form of service should be introduced into Scottish churches led Scottish ministers and lawyers to draw up the National Covenant to defend not only the church, but also Scottish institutions and laws against English domination. It was signed by nobles and gentlemen in Greyfriars Church, Edinburgh, in 1638 and copies were then circulated to every town and shire in Scotland for signing.

When it appeared that the Covenanters were getting ready to create a government of their own, the King sent forces against them which led to a civil war, later to engulf the whole of Britain, and to the invasion of England by the Scots, who occupied Newcastle. In Scotland itself, the Marquis of Montrose led a Highland army on the King's side but was defeated and later executed.
After the execution of Charles I himself and the defeat of the Scots by Cromwell, Charles II landed in Scotland and accepted the terms of the Covenant in a bid to regain his throne, which was eventually restored to him in 1660. The Convenanters had tried but failed to impose a rigid religious control over Scotland, and although they eventually alienated many who had signed the Convenant, support for them continued in isolated pockets of the country for more than a century.

DALRIADA: A 6th-century Kingdom established on the west side of Scotland by the Irish Scots, led by King Fergus.

ELL: This was the old Scottish linear measurement whose standard was kept at Edinburgh. One ell equalled $3\frac{1}{12}$ ft (33.5 cm).

GAELIC: Gaelic was, and still is, particularly in the Western islands of Scotland, the mother tongue of the Highlanders. This Celtic language has close affinities with the Irish language, and is distantly related to Welsh.

JACOBITE REBELLIONS: The Jacobite rebellions were a series of four different Scottish rebellions, spanning the years from 1708 to 1745, aimed at restoring the Stewart Kings to the British throne and involving three generations of this dynasty.
The Jacobites were the supporters of James II & VII, who reigned from 1685 until 1689, when he lost his throne, and of his son, also called James, better known as the Old Pretender. Bonnie Prince Charlie, the Young

Pretender, James II's grandson, brought the Jacobite cause to full and romantic flowering in the 1745 rising.

1708: First Jacobite Rising. The French King, having given sanctuary to the Stewarts, who set up a court at Saint Germain (where the exiled James II & VII died in 1701), sent a fleet to Scotland with 6,000 men and James' son, the Old Pretender (or James III & VIII as the Jacobites preferred to call their "King over the water"). It headed for the Firth of Forth and Edinburgh but bad weather prevented a .

1715: Second Jacobite Rising. Historians now suggest that this second rebellion actually had a better chance of succeeding than the more dramatic and romantic cause of Bonnie Prince Charlie 30 years later. The Hanoverian line which had succeeded Queen Anne (half-sister to the Old Pretender), the last of the Stewart monarchs to reign, was unpopular and unstable, and in Scotland itself the Act of Union uniting England and Scotland in 1707 had still not been wholly accepted.
Led by the 11th Earl of Mar, and supported by Cameron of Lochiel and others, the Royal Standard of the Stewarts was raised at Braemar on 6 September. By the end of the month, Mar had occupied Inverness and Perth and controlled the eastern coastline with 12,000 men. But by the time James, the Old Pretender, landed at Peterhead at the beginning of December, the army, in retreat from Argyll's smaller forces, had begun to melt away as it marched north, and the towns had rallied to the Hanoverian government. Two months later, with no help forthcoming from the French, the Old Pretender and Mar sailed back to France.

1719: Third Jacobite Rising. This was a very minor affair, initiated by the French, for European diplomatic reasons, rather than the Scots. Two French frigates and several hundred men under the command of the Earl Marischal, who had been involved in the 1715 Rising, sailed to the north-west of Scotland. After calling in at the island of Lewis, they established their mainland base at Eilean Donan Castle on Loch Duich but gained few Scottish supporters and were routed in Glen Shiel.

1745: Fourth Jacobite Rising. This, the most famous of them all, owes much to the charismatic personality of the Young Pretender, 23-year-old Prince Charles Edward Stewart, who led a

Scottish army almost as far as London before being defeated at Culloden in 1746. His defeat was partially due to the many changes that had taken place in the 30 years since 1715, not least the roads built for military traffic in the Highlands by General Wade and the raising of Highland regiments, such as the Black Watch, by the government to siphon off Highland manpower.

Recalled by Louis XV from Rome, where the Stewarts had been forced to seek refuge with the Pope, Prince Charles Edward had hoped for French support, but in the end had to pawn his jewels and borrow money to buy arms.

On 23 July, 1745, he landed at Moidart in the West Highlands, with only seven men, three of whom were Irish and one English. At first, the clan chiefs like Macdonald of Clanranald, on whose territory the Prince had landed, Macdonald of Sleat and Macleod of Dunvegan, refused to join him. But after Lochiel, chief of the Camerons, was won over, rather against his judgement, other clans gathered around him. When the Royal Standard was raised at Glenfinnan the Prince had only 1,000 men, but the numbers grew as clans like the Stewarts of Appin, the Macphersons, Robertsons and the Atholl men joined him.

Bonnie Prince Charlie held court at the Palace of Holyrood in Edinburgh before beginning his advance into England at the end of October, reaching Derby by 4 December, a remarkably short space of time. King George II was preparing to flee the capital and Londoners were terrified, but as the government forces began to rally, the Prince was advised to withdraw and the retreat back to Scotland began.

That retreat culminated in the bloody Battle of Culloden, near Inverness, in 1746, which spelt not just the end of the Jacobite cause, but the start of the break-up, not only of the clans, but of the whole social and economic structure of the Highlands. What followed were the mass emigrations to the New World and the clearances of the crofting communities to make way for sheep and sporting estates, a terrible loss of population which Highlanders in Scotland and expatriates mourn to this day.

KEEP: A tall, fortified Scottish tower house.

KILT: Pleated lengths of tartan cloth, reaching to the knees, part of Highland male dress (see BREACAN-FEILE).

LEINE–CHROICH: The Gaelic word for a loose shirt stopping short just above the knee which the Irish wore, marked with stripes to show rank, and thought to be the precursor of the tartan kilt.

LYON COURT: Scotland's court of heraldry, which also has the legal status to rule upon rightful holders of hereditary titles and clan chiefships, as well as matriculating (registering) arms, crests and tartans.

PHILLABEG (FILLABEG): The little kilt as opposed to the belted plaid (See explanation under BREACAN-FEILE).

PLAID: A rectangular length of woollen cloth, usually tartan, which was formerly an outer garment (See BREACAN-FEILE) and later became the word for a woman's shawl. Nowadays, it is part of the ceremonial dress of the pipe bands of Scottish regiments.

PONTIFICAL: A bishop's office-book.

REIVER: Robber, or more often in the Scottish context, cattle-rustler, particularly the case with the Border reivers.

RUNRIG: System of land tenure in single holdings made up of small, detached pieces.

SEPT: Branch or division of a clan.

SETT: A checked pattern in cloth, particularly the arrangement of squares and stripes in a tartan.

SKEAN DHU: The Highlander's short-bladed sheath-knife or dirk, now commonly worn in the stocking as part of Highland dress.

SPORRAN: The leather purse or pouch worn in front of a man's kilt.

STRATH: A river valley.

SLOGANS & WAR CRIES: The clan slogans, like their war-cries, were means of identification, used particularly in the heat of battle or at night. They were also used on more peaceful occasions, like clan gatherings or tournaments, as a bond of brotherhood.

The actual slogans themselves were often the names of geographical features of the clan homelands, such as mountains, like the Campbells' Cruachan, or the names of past heroes, like the Macleans' war-cry, *"Fear eil' air son Eachainn!"* — "Another for Hector" — recalling the loyalty of the clansmen to their chief in the Battle of Inverkeithing.

Some slogans have been registered with the Lord Lyon King of Arms, who has allowed them as secondary clan mottoes. If they are used on public occasions without having been allowed by the Lord Lyon a breach of the peace charge could be laid against the user.

TACK: A lease or tenancy, particularly of a farm or mill. The tacksman was the leaseholder.

TARGE: A light shield.

TARTAN REGISTRATION: The Lord Lyon, Scotland's King of Arms with his own legal court, has no jurisdiction over who wears which tartans. The Lyon Court maintains a register of tartans, although only clan chiefs, the heads of ancient families, and, in exceptional circumstances, public bodies, are allowed to register their tartans, authenticating the colours and count of the sett.

As Mr. Malcolm Innes of Edingight, the Lord Lyon, points out, new tartans are not granted lightly. Several Canadian provinces, such as Nova Scotia, New Brunswick and Newfoundland, have their tartans registered, as well as America's West Point Military Academy.

Only some 40 clan tartans are actually registered with the Lord Lyon. These include Cameron, clan Chattan, Farquharson, Grant, Innes, McBain, Macdonald of Clanranald, McFarlane, Mackenzie, Mackinnon, Rose, Sinclair and Thomson. On the other hand, the Scottish Tartans Society of Comrie, Perthshire, has over 1500 tartans on its list of registrations, with new ones constantly being added.

THANE: A noble with certain powers of jurisdiction over a tract of land.

THANAGE: The jurisdiction of the thane.

TREWS: Close-fitting trousers, usually made of tartan and often worn by Scottish regiments.

VASSAL: A holder of heritable property who paid feu duty to a superior.